LIFT!

going up if teaching gets you down

39 reflections to promote resilience and well-being

David Gumbrell

First published in 2019 by Critical Publishing Ltd

British Library Cataloguing in Publication Data
A CIP record for this book is available from the British Library

ISBN: 978-1-912508-48-8

This book is also available in the following e-book formats:

MOBI ISBN: 978-1-912508-49-5
EPUB ISBN: 978-1-912508-50-1
Adobe e-book ISBN: 978-1-912508-51-8

The right of David Gumbrell to be identified as the Author of this work has been asserted by him in accordance with the Copyright, Design and Patents Act 1988.

Cartoon illustrations by Élisabeth Eudes-Pascal represented by GCI

Cover and text design by Out of House Limited
Project Management by Newgen Publishing UK
Printed and bound in Great Britain by 4edge, Essex

Critical Publishing
3 Connaught Road
St Albans
AL3 5RX

www.criticalpublishing.com

Paper from responsible sources

ENDORSEMENTS

Lift! is a joy to read – a valuable book to dip in and out of throughout any teacher's career! Full of fascinating facts, engaging ideas and thought-provoking reflections, the chapters provide a treasure trove for any teacher who is striving to retain the essential professional sparkle needed in a resilient teacher.

Professor Anna Lise Gordon, Director of the Institute of Education at St Mary's University, Twickenham

This is the book that needed to be written. I found it fun to read, full of inspirational, engaging ideas linked to real life, which will help you if you are a new teacher, or if you are more established, to adopt 39 brilliant strategies to support your inner resilience. I am thrilled to endorse David Gumbrell as the 'Resilience Man' as his transformational ideas will support your self-belief and enthuse you to do even-more amazing things with pupils.

Dr Neil Hawkes, Founder, VBE International

Reading *Lift!* reminded me of another great book that I once read about connecting with the soul, finding one's purpose and becoming our Personal Legend. Not unlike the Alchemist in Paul Coelho's book, David shows us here how to find the treasure in teaching and how you only truly find it when you do not give up. Resilience is a trait in the best teachers, the ones who both know and understand how to adapt and how real impact can only ever be measured over time. Honing the craft of teaching takes time, patience and self-belief.

Taking the time to reflect and understand yourself is the key to happiness in teaching and what spurs us on. Being yourself and understanding that there is no one right way to teach is fundamental. Equally fundamental is having the resources to support you on the journey. *Lift!* is a wonderful companion to those moments when you are not sure which colleague, friend, pedagogical theory or teaching resource to turn to. It is the satnav to guide you when you become unsure of the way and offers support to show you that you can do it and overcome hurdles. Ultimately this will give you the strength to see that at times when you may be unsure or overwhelmed.

Teaching is a wonderful job, the best of jobs, but it can feel lonely and there are times when every teacher feels down. Understanding ways to look after yourself and the importance of pausing in order to get back up is what this book will do and the gentle humour, wit and elevating expression will not fail to lift you!

Nicola McEwan, Director of ITT, University of Buckingham

Inspiring and valuing our teachers of today to be the philosophers of the future. Take time out to read these engaging, quirky and insightful reflections to strengthen your professional and personal well-being.

Jo Munn, Deputy Director of Education, Diocese of Gloucester

When you're on a plane they ask you to put your own oxygen mask on first because they recognise you have to be in a fit state to help others. It's the same with teaching – self-care needs to come first to enable teachers to help others. This book contains a wealth of ideas and strategies to help teachers look after themselves better.

Dr Edward Sellman, Centre for Research in Human Flourishing, University of Nottingham

David's deep professional concern to keep teachers teaching is a hallmark of this book. The book offers engaging practical strategies that come from a lively and knowledgeable understanding of the demands of the profession and the demands teachers make of themselves. I would encourage new and established teachers to use David's ideas to reflect on their resilience

Matthew Sossick, Deputy Director and Head of Initial Teacher Education, University of Roehampton

THEMATIC INDEX

The chapters in LIFT! can be read sequentially or the content can be dipped into as needed. The following categories will help you find your way through the book if you have a specific problem or worry. Each category is identified by an icon, which also appears in the contents listing and at the start of each chapter to help you identify the chapters you need and navigate your way through the book.

ARE YOU FEELING THAT YOU...

... have lost your way?

GET A LIFT WITH CHAPTERS 9, 21, 30, 34 AND 39.

... need to pause, or stop?

GET A LIFT WITH CHAPTERS 1, 4, 5, 12, 14, 24, 25 AND 29.

... have lost perspective?

GET A LIFT WITH CHAPTERS 2, 7, 13, 16, 22, 26 AND 34.

... need to reconnect with others?

GET A LIFT WITH CHAPTERS 6, 10, 18, 20, 33 AND 37.

... are pushing yourself too far?

GET A LIFT WITH CHAPTERS 3, 15, 17, 19, 32, 35 AND 36.

... have an impossible problem to solve?

GET A LIFT WITH CHAPTERS 8, 11, 23, 27, 28, 31 AND 38.

To Julie, Fiona and Sue

who boost my resilience when I need it most.

Our titles are also available in a range of electronic formats. To order, or for details of our bulk discounts, please go to our website www.criticalpublishing.com or contact our distributor, NBN International, 10 Thornbury Road, Plymouth PL6 7PP, telephone 01752 202301 or e-mail orders@nbninternational.com.

CONTENTS

 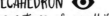

CONTENTS

CONTENTS

FOREWORD

As a mental health nurse with over 30 years experience working within the mental health sector I have had the privilege to work towards changing the world for people who are affected by mental health difficulties whether as a sufferer, a carer, a teacher or a mental health professional. Every role I have held has led me further along this amazing and insightful journey.

Throughout my 30-plus years I have met many inspiring individuals and have observed a common factor within the mental health community that ties us together – we all want to make a positive difference.

Meeting David was like a meeting of the minds – two people from different professional backgrounds but with a common goal: to support the development of emotional resilience and through doing so improve the mental health and well-being of generations to come. No small task, but if anyone is up for the job it's David!

In his book *Lift!* David Gumbrell writes in a truly engaging style which provides the reader with helpful tips and goals to support the building of their own emotional resilience.

David gives access to a variety of accessible 'recipes' to realise self-awareness and personal reflection that gently leads you on a voyage of discovery that cannot help but result in personal growth and enhanced emotional resilience – essential ingredients for thriving in today's modern world.

It is essential to care for oneself in order to be able to care effectively for others. Just as when we fly we are reminded to apply our own oxygen mask before helping others with theirs, we need to be reminded to care for our own emotional well-being so that we can help others in their journey.

David gives us permission to do just that – self-care and self-emotional nurturing is not selfish it is as essential to our health as the air we breathe and the food we eat.

This is not a run-of-the-mill self-help book – it's fun, innovative, original and inspiring and it will take you one step further to changing the world!

Kate Majid, RMN, CEO Shaw Mind Foundation

David Gumbrell

I am an educational consultant, working in schools to support teachers with their resilience and also with teacher training providers and student teachers. I deliver INSET days and one-to-one coaching sessions, and I also speak at headteacher conferences. Drawing on more than 20 years of teaching experience, including seven years as a headteacher, and research conducted at Kingston University, I feel I am well placed to nurture the development of those new to the profession as well as those who have been teaching for a little longer! I am passionate about teacher well-being and resilience but also understand how precious time is for teachers and wanted to create a resource that made the best use of this.

INTRODUCTION: ARISE, CARAT CAKE

How to attain that much-needed LIFT!

- **Does anyone have a good recipe for carrot cake?**

Or

- **Does anyone have a recipe for a 'carat cake'?**

The judges will be scoring it on carat (weight), cut, clarity and colour. These four criteria are usually used in judging the quality of diamonds and yet they could be used to judge a baking competition – we all use 'diamonds' whenever we bake a cake!

Self-raising flour is added to the butter, eggs and sugar. This key final ingredient allows the cake to rise. It differs from plain flour in that it includes the raising agents needed to allow the cake to increase in size during baking. Despite making up only 5 per cent of self-raising flour, these raising agents (which include the key ingredient of cream of tartar) are crucial. Cream of tartar sounds a lot more appealing than tartaric acid, but essentially they are the same. By adding 'cream', it sounds quintessentially

English, while adding 'acid' to a cake sounds more likely to be part of the plot of an obscure murder mystery set at a village fete.

It transpires that this humble ingredient is a naturally produced derivative of grape fermentation; indeed, it is the primary acidic flavour that we taste (and many of us enjoy) in wine. More prevalent in white wine than red, the tartaric compounds crystallise, even within the bottle. The crystals form on the underside of the cork and are nicknamed by vintners as 'wine diamonds'. So, when you bake a cake, you really are adding cut, clarity, colour and carat.

Your showstopper creation, thanks to the bubble-creating acid that you measured out so carefully, is now ready for judging; its addition has helped the cake to rise. In a similar way there might be occasions when you need something that acts as an agent to raise your spirits. Your daily toils can be difficult and sometimes challenging. You need to seek ways to 'lighten your texture' and to give yourself that timely mental boost when you are feeling the heat. This is essentially what resilience is – your ability to manage your everyday thoughts, feelings and emotions.

You may well have your own recipe for how to achieve this. For you, it might be a walk in the park combined with coffee with a friend and decorated with a sprinkle of box-set watching. On other days, you may commend to yourself a reheat of a favourite book, a simmer in the bath before glazing over for a good night's rest. Whatever your baking prowess, you need to ensure that you include them all in your mix – the mix of your experiences, thoughts and moods. Like everyone else, you are an emotional being who needs to alleviate the demands of everyday life.

In this book, I offer you 39 strategies for resilience. These include ideas to provoke thought, reminders of vital ingredients, and conversational 'slices' to share with others. Each chapter attempts to provide a timely LIFT! of your emotions. Dip in for a single portion, or dive into a regular diet of mental nutrition.

Intended to promote reflection and personal contemplation, I hope that the content will allow you to become ever more self-raising; able to rise to the challenges of everyday life and become increasingly more resilient as a result of reading the book. By sifting through the words held within these chapters, you can make your understanding of resilience ever more refined.

David Gumbrell

I. SOPORIFIC SCRABBLE SCORE ⓫

The value of developing soporific conditions

- **Can you think of a five-letter word that *does not* contain the letter 'e'?**

  It is harder now that I've said not to include the 'e' as it makes you think of exactly that!

- **What about a word that does not have either an 'e' or a 't' within it?**

  This is a little harder, isn't it?

- **Would you still be using the same word if I ask for a five-letter word without an 'e', 't' or 'a'?**

  This limits it further.

- **Why these three letters?**

  Well, 'e', 't' and 'a' are the most frequently used letters in the Oxford English Dictionary; therefore, you are likely to rummage more in your mental lexicon to find a word to match the criteria.

Indeed, basic ciphers use letter displacement to encrypt 'secret' messages. Intended, like all codes, to be unbreakable, they are quite the reverse as the solution lies in the frequency of the letters in the English language. Due to the prevalence of the letter 'e', any equivalent symbol would also occur most frequently. You can then translate that across to the 'coded' message and its 'secret' will be revealed soon enough.

Board games too, such as the popular Scrabble, have a letter distribution that matches the frequency of each letter. However, their values reflect this too and thus the 'e' scores a measly one point, whereas a 'k' or a 'j' would score you five or eight points, respectively.

So, taking your five-letter word earlier, and without bonuses for its placement on a Scrabble board, what score would you get for it? Eight? Twelve? Fifteen?

However, the word 'soporific' in the title would score zero in Scrabble (as a starter word). Do you know why? It scores zero as it is a nine-letter word and Scrabble only allows for seven starter tiles per player, doesn't it? To include this word, you would have to add 'porific' to a 'so' that had already been played on the board.

While it may have a limited Scrabble value, it has greater value in its meaning. Soporific means 'sleep inducing'. Basically, anything that helps to support you in getting to sleep would be classed as soporific and so has enormous real-term value. This is important, as the quality of your sleep is the prime indicator of your resilience. Without sleep, or with poor sleep, it does not take long before you are no longer able to function efficiently or effectively.

Research suggests that adults need between seven and nine hours of sleep a night, or a 'sleep debt' is created (that will have to be 'paid off' with a lie-in at the weekend). To prepare for sleep you need to be incorporating 'soporific' moments to ready yourself for this most restorative of processes.

Beatrix Potter suggested that eating lettuce was soporific for 'Flopsy Bunnies', but for humans, recommendations include other things. These include:

- **no caffeine after midday;**
- **no mobile devices or television an hour before going to bed;**
- **exercise during the day;**
- **reduction of light in the room;**
- **stick to a regular sleep schedule.**

You could try alcohol, as this does have soporific qualities, but unfortunately, these effects are short-lived and do not sustain sleep once induced. Your overall night's sleep would be significantly disrupted.

You need to find what works for you, but what is clear is that you need to do more to promote good sleep and to prepare your body by winding down to get ready for it, rather than switching off the mobile device, turning over and attempting to fall asleep straight away!

2. SNAKES. NOT LADDERS 👁

Gain an accurate perception of your day, your week, your year

The game of Snakes and Ladders has a surprisingly moral-driven history. It first originated in India where the snakes punished you for being sinful, whereas ladders celebrated more virtuous attributes. Interestingly, in this first edition, there were more snakes than there were ladders, I guess in a drive to demonstrate to young Indian children what not to do, rather than promoting good choices.

In its European counterpart, some centuries later, the number of ladders and snakes were equalised, maybe in an attempt by Victorians (since they first brought the game to the UK) to create a more balanced approach to character education for the children it was aimed at. Insolence, poverty and illness were inevitable slides down a slippery snake – whereas charity, goodwill and dignity were promotions up a few rungs of a ladder.

House rules, variants of the game that we played as modern children, included the inevitable final dice rolls – that precarious final dash from 91 to 100. Four squares away from the finish, you finally throw a six, aargh! Square 98 is a snake and you 'count back' if you don't get the exact number. Did you use that rule? Or were you slightly more forgiving (as we are talking about values and virtues) and allowed for the exact number only throw or, even better, 'at least' dice rules to get you beyond the magic 100 square?

Apart from the inevitable link to 'bounce-back-ability' of that final dice throw, the game of Snakes and Ladders can be a useful mental image to call upon in both good times and bad. Just like our Victorian ancestors, we all have days that go well, and days that don't. Some weeks go well, others, less so. A morning can be a struggle and a battle, but the day picks up in the afternoon. I'm sure that you've had these combinations and more.

But, no matter whether it's your day, your week, your month or your year, you have more control than you think when it comes to your perception of that time and place. If you accept that you, like all human beings, are imperfect and vulnerable (and that the day is going to contain both snakes and ladders) then you can adjust your expectations accordingly. This reality check means that you can almost prepare for some snakes, or at least limit their effect on you. Rather than dwelling at the bottom of a snake, feeling sorry for yourself, you can set your mind to acknowledge that it was a dip, rather than a trend. Can't you?

Teachers are notoriously good at chastening themselves, like those playing the Indian and Victorian variants of Snakes and Ladders were doing. But, no matter how long you dwell at the bottom of a snake, try spending an equal time at the top of a ladder. Pat yourself on the back for the same length of time as you offer self-criticism and self-judgement.

This more balanced perception of reality is a far cry from what most teachers do. Just as the Victorians balanced off the number of snakes and ladders from the Indian version, why don't you try to reduce the size of the snakes and ladders themselves and level off the highs, as well as the lows, of your teaching day, your week, your year?

- **Just spend a few minutes now thinking back to something that you have recently done well. When you recall it, give yourself a metaphorical 'pat on the back' – it will feel good.**

3. DOBBY DOUBTS ⏱

Don't become overly critical of yourself

- **Did you know that the character of Dobby appears in five of the seven Harry Potter books and yet only appeared in two of the films?**

Also, do you know...

- **In which book did the character of Dobby first appear?**
- **What was Dobby trying to stop Harry from doing in his home?**
- **When Harry refused to take Dobby's advice, what did he make hover?**

Read on and see if you are right.

During his first appearance in *Harry Potter and the Chamber of Secrets*, the sock-loving character of Dobby, with his eyes the *size of tennis balls*, became a popular characterisation of the feelings of guilt and subsequent admonishment. While we all make mistakes, J K Rowling's three-foot-tall character takes the area of self-punishment to a whole new level. From shutting his ears in the oven door for coming to see Harry in the second book of the series, we read from the start that this character is prone to guilt, shame and public chastisement.

While initially comical, there is a darker undertone that becomes apparent as the reader works their way through the rest of the books in the series. After all, Dobby's arrival at Privet Drive is well intentioned and is aimed at preventing Harry from returning to Hogwarts and becoming further embroiled in the magical goings-on there. In an act of desperation (or indeed of punishment for Harry's non-compliance) Dobby then uses a hover spell to get Harry 'told off' by the Dursleys for using magic out of context. Aunt Petunia's 'masterpiece pudding' is levitated by Dobby to achieve this! For every action there is a reaction, and thus Harry is locked in his room with seemingly no escape (well at least until the start of Chapter 3).

We all make mistakes – they are part of being the imperfect human beings that we all are – but we all differ in the ways we react to those mistakes.

- **When is a mistake simply that, a mistake?**
- **Can a mistake be a deliberate act, or does it need to be accidental?**
- **How do you differentiate between a deliberate act and an accidental one?**
- **Or can you blame it on Harry Potter magic?**

Your perception of what is a 'worthy self-punishment' is likely to depend on your confidence at the time, your self-esteem in that moment and also the reaction of the person who is affected by the 'mistake'. It is unavoidably contextual to your moods and your feelings, and the people around you. When you are at a low ebb, you are more likely to be over-critical, possibly judgemental, and more likely to be irrational in your responses to mistakes.

With this in mind, you need to calibrate your reaction when things go wrong and encourage others to help you to gauge it when it does. In a similar way to Harry, you need to surround yourself with your own Hermiones and Rons. They supported him throughout the series, whereas the self-harming Dobby is rather isolated from his house-elf peers and therefore doesn't have the same outlet for his feelings, emotions and actions.

As a teacher you need to try and be less critical of yourself. Realise that mistakes are inevitable, normal and to be expected. Rather than dwell on the things that don't go well, consider the majority that do! You would also do well to surround yourself with people who can support you in generating a more positive outlook.

4. A COUP FOR CHICKENS ⏸

The importance of sleep for your overall resilience

- **What comes into your mind when I say the word chicken?**

    1) Sage and onion stuffing?

    2) Nuggets and ketchup?

    3) Free-range, or battery?

    4) Sleep?

Yes, sleep! Usually the only animal that we connect with sleep is sheep! Counting sheep jumping over the proverbial fence. One sheep, two sheep... one thousand sheep... sleep!

But domestic chickens sit within a very exclusive club (with dolphins, seals and birds) in that they can perform something called uni-hemispheric sleep. Put in simple terms, this means that they can sleep half their brain, while the other half can stay awake and alert. This apparent superpower is a superb adaptation. Scientists still differ in their opinion as to why they have it or how it was bequeathed to them. But however this ability came to them, there is now an agreement within the scientific community that they do actually have it.

It certainly gives them advantages in terms of survival as it allows them to be on continuous alert for predators. It increases the proportion of time that they can have 'one eye open sleep' at times of risk and then have a deeper 'two-eyed sleep' at times when they are feeling less threatened. Before you get too jealous, it is not that they don't need sleep, more that they have extra flexibility in when they get that deeper restorative sleep that we all need in order to fully function.

But no creature can go without sleep for a prolonged period of time as it is too important. The body cannot last long without sleep before it suffers detrimental health effects as a result. In fact, the 1964 Guinness World Record for sleep deprivation (held by the American Randy Gardner) stands at 11 days and 25 minutes! This record will continue to stand, as Guinness no longer registers sleep deprivation records as it is felt that it is too damaging to the human body to do so.

In the pecking order of things that have the greatest impact on resilience, it is known that the quality of sleep comes out on top. Despite admiring the superpowered chickens, dolphins and seals, you need to consider your own ability to do something about getting your own sleep patterns working for you personally. You need:

- **sufficient sleep to allow you to rise in the morning feeling refreshed;**
- **enough sleep to not be reliant on caffeine in the mornings;**
- **regular and ample sleep that amounts to a 'sleep routine'.**

It is known that even slightly limited sleep can make your decision-making less rational, can make you more irritable and increasingly prone to mood swings. This in turn can lead you to becoming less productive, resulting in tasks taking you a lot longer than they should. In an attempt to kick-start yourself, you may sometimes fuel up on stimulants to help you to get up to the speed that you need to be in order to function efficiently.

- **Do you repeat this on a daily basis in a vain attempt to maintain the status quo?**
- **Are these habits more prevalent during term time?**

Furthermore, you may attempt to increase the 'window of opportunity' by staying up later and getting up ever earlier, yet work becomes progressively ineffective when you do. Indeed, you can even become prone to mental lapses in your attention span – which can manifest itself as 'nodding off' and that is not productive at all!

Overall, you need to find what works for you. However, starting tonight, maybe you should stop counting sheep and start to count chickens instead!

- **Just spend a few minutes now thinking about your 'sleep routine'.**
- **What does that routine already include?**
- **What do you need to add to it in order to make it more effective?**

5. NYCTINASTIC AT NIGHT ⬛

What you can learn from plants that gradually close at night

- **Apart from being plants, what do water lilies, daisies and crocuses have in common?**

They could all be classed as 'nasty' plants – ones that are able to react to light, temperature, arrival of insects and to touch. The most famous 'nastic movement' – hence the suffix 'nasty' – is that of the Venus fly trap. This capacity, called 'thigmo-nasty', gives these plants the ability to close their leaves in around 100 milliseconds! Unfortunately, neither lilies, daisies, nor crocuses are touch-sensitive in this way, nor are they able to make such dramatic and speedy changes to their structure!

However, nycti-nasty (note again the 'nasty' suffix ending), is induced by diurnal variations in both light and temperature, which is a common trait in all the flowers listed above. In simple terms, this means that the petals are controlled by the changes between night and day. Ancient Egyptians were fascinated by this capability in the lotus flower (what we call a water lily). They were charmed by the fact that it closed at night and opened again in the morning. Indeed, they attributed this to the power of the Sun-God, Amun-Ra, and thus lotus flowers were used as a symbol of God-like powers. Water lilies were used to decorate walls inside pyramids, adorn the tops of important pillars and embellish important papyrus, indicating their significance.

Just like dawn and dusk are the transitions between light and dark, sun and no-sun, there is a similar, graduated transition between open and closed for these impressive plants. This is a gradual change – a phase that takes time – rather than an immediate switch between the two.

But, no matter what works for you in terms of sleep preparation, you need to become more consciously aware of the importance of the transitionary period towards sleep. Rather than pretending that you don't need to go through this phase, you would be wise to build it into your daily schedule.

- **Do you expect too much of your brain to be 'fully functioning' when answering emails until ten at night, and then 'switching yourself off' minutes later?**

- **Do you shine the light of a television into your eyes, subjecting yourself to fast-paced, ever-changing images for your brain to process, and yet still expect your brain to be ready for sleep soon after the programme is finished?**

Just like plants being sensitive to light, temperature and touch, you also need to identify for yourself the triggers that make you 'sleep sensitive'. When you yawn, you need to take that as a bodily signal for needing sleep and subsequently do something about it, rather than ignoring it. It doesn't have to be straightaway but take it as a sign that you need to wind down.

Plants seem to have 'sleep sensitivity' as an algorithmic function, but do we?

- **Do you need to listen to your body more carefully in order to sense the environmental triggers that prompt you to rest?**

- **Are you willing to over-ride these bodily sleep triggers in order to comply to a sub-culture where it has become mainstream to do exactly this?**

- **What are the signs and symptoms, for you, that make you aware that your body needs to rest and to sleep?**

- **In practical terms what could you do to change your night-time habits and transition better to sleep?**

6. OTTER AND OTTER

Keep yourself anchored like sea otters do

- What connects Dead Man's Fingers, Creep Horn and Landlady's Wig?
- Which ingredient is used as a thickening agent in ice cream, toothpaste and hair conditioners?

The answer to the first question is that they are the common names that have been given to three varieties of the 10,000 different seaweeds identified in Britain and Ireland. In answer to the second question, products that are harnessed from seaweed are used in more products than we would first believe. Known as a fertiliser (isn't it seaweed that makes Jersey potatoes so tasty?), it is also used for cooking (the popularity of sushi has highlighted this) but also for 'bathroom products', which is less well known.

Many seaweeds (kelp) use two key adaptations to survive. The first is the 'holdfast'. Unlike the cryptic names of the seaweeds at the start, the holdfast does exactly what its name suggests it would do. It is the mechanism that anchors the algae to the ocean floor. It is the attachment to the rock that keeps it in the same place – gently swaying with the tidal ebbs and flows.

The second built-in feature is that kelp have air-filled sacs (called bladders) that allow them to float in the water. They are therefore able to create underwater 'streamers' rising from the sea bed to the water level.

This acts as a perfect way for sea otters to keep themselves in one place while they catch up on some sleep! By entwining the kelp around their arms or legs, they are able to tie themselves up for the night and therefore not float away too far from where they want to be. Put simply, the seaweed has a holdfast system that the sea otter borrows! What an ingenious idea. Maybe you could learn something from these sea-otters.

- **How could you anchor yourself in turbulent times?**
- **How do you remain buoyant?**

In times of need, you (like everyone else) need the support of others. Resilience is not a one-person task. You need to be regulated by those around you, someone to give you that timely boost of 'You're great', or 'Really, is that all you are worried about?', or 'Try this, it might work, it does for me'. These words (if timed well) are so important – especially if they come from the right person at the right time and in the right way. If they do, then they can be a vital anchor in stormy times.

Holdfasts are physical attachment to rocks, and yet being a 'rock for someone' is more about emotional attachment and being in tune with that other person. Their empathetic stance offers a mental safe haven for either exploring the issue or distracting you from it. Either way you can rest easy in the rock's company, knowing that you are going to 'be OK' – just like the sea otter's ability to rest up and sleep!

So, to remain buoyant, you can't do it alone. Sea otters 'pair up' and you need to do the same. You need to nurture trust in your relationships so that they can build over time. You have to be willing to 'give and take' in a mutually beneficial, two-way connection. If you do this then you can be anchored, buoyant, held-fast and therefore more resilient as a result!

Reflect for a moment about:

- **Who is your 'holdfast'?**
- **Who keeps you buoyant?**
- **Who is your anchor?**

My challenge is now for you to tell them that they play this vital role for you!

7. THE MANY FACES OF A DODECAHEDRON

Consider things from different perspectives - from all 'faces'

Come and meet the family of shapes called Platonic solids which, apart from all being named after the Greek mathematician Plato, have one other thing in common: they are all 3D shapes that consist of repeated, regular 2D shapes.

The first of the two smallest members of the family, named tetrahedron, is made up of four (as the prefix tetra would suggest) equilateral triangles. To many, the four triangles form a pyramid, although the Ancient Egyptians preferred the square-based versions of the shape (and thus couldn't be part of this Platonic grouping). The second, most well-known shape, is the cube, which is formed of six squares and used most often in board games as dice!

Their older cousin, who might have an octopus for a pet, is the next triangle-based shape named octahedron. This shape consists of eight equilateral triangles. Imagine two pyramids (the Egyptian, square-based ones) stuck together, by their bases, and you have a profile picture of this family member!

Looking more ball-like, and not too dissimilar to Channel 4's 'Crystal Maze' dome, the fourth member of our family is a 20-triangle shape. This more complex construction has a name to match, icosahedron ('icos' meaning 20 in Greek). Such stature would warrant the slightly eccentric uncle of the family.

Our final member, arguably the grandad of the family, is the dodecahedron and if it were a dice, then it would need the numbers 1 to 12 on it as there are a dozen regular pentagon faces that construct his form.

Each member of this Platonic family that have been presented to you have a unique set of characteristics that make them who they are. Although they may share the same triangular constituent parts, tetrahedron, octahedron and icosahedron are all different. In a similar way, your own family (indeed, your friends and colleagues too) are all unique and different. In fact, it is their diversity that allows them to bring such a wealth of support into your life. Collectively, thanks to them, you are who you are and as a result you are stronger because of them.

Resilience is not about fighting on in solitude. That is an outdated definition that does not serve us well here. Rather you have a network of people who you can turn to, text, email and call when you need them most. However, in your busy life, you may not be able to catch these people and therefore you need to consider alternatives. On reflection, I believe that you can infer what someone would say to you if you put yourself in their shoes. If they were present, watching you in the situation:

- **How would they react?**
- **What would they advise?**
- **What would they say?**

Take a moment to imagine a die. It has not got symbols, numbers or colours on it. Instead it has names on each of the faces. Each surface has a loved one, a valued colleague, or a role model etched into it. When you struggle in a situation, you could bring out this die, roll it and then consider how that person would advise you. This is not a replacement for that person; rather it is more something supplementary to them when they are not present. Consider it as an interim measure, an initial support mechanism that might be helpful.

Reflect now on the people who would appear on your die. Maybe you have two dice, one for home life, the other for work. Whatever works for you. Consider the 'faces' to go on your personal dice.

- **Who are the six people you would include?**

8. A WORKING FACTORIAL

How adding an exclamation mark can make a big difference!

WHAAM! POW! KABOOM! SPLAT!

- **The one-word sentences above are all staples from comic books where action-packed heroes have got themselves into yet another scrape with their arch-enemy or nemesis.**

They are so familiar and an intrinsic part of our childhood. One theory that pervades the internet is that the use of exclamation marks in comic books was to do with the quality of the printing process and that the full stop frequently wasn't printed. To compensate, the exclamation mark was added as it was more likely to print. Do you buy into this theory? I think that it was more to do with the speed of the action that was taking place and how there was limited space to convey this within a speech bubble.

Unknown by some, the exclamation mark is also used in maths. If you add an exclamation mark to the end of the number three (ie 3!) then that becomes what is called 'three factorial'. In short, this means that it is $3 \times 2 \times 1$, which equals 6.

If you then calculate 4! you get $4 \times 3 \times 2 \times 1 = 24$

It doesn't take long until this sequence creates numbers that exceed a million. In fact, '10!' is over three and a half million, so they grow at quite a pace.

Indeed, such is the rise in the numbers that it is a common belief that when you have completed a shuffle of a pack of playing cards they will end up being in a unique order, a combination that has never been created before. I am not sure that anyone would need to, or indeed want to check this for real, but statistically this is true. So, maybe you can impress someone with your new 'mathe-magical' trick?

- **If you combined your newly found mathematical knowledge by adding an exclamation mark to everyday words, could you magnify them exponentially too?**

For example, in terms of meeting your physical needs you could 'walk!' rather 'walk'. A walk once a week can build to twice a week, then to three times a week, etc. That increases it to something more than it previously was. By walking, you can match the mental demands of teaching with more physical demands that can help your resilience.

Alternatively, in order to meet your intellectual needs, you could 'read!' rather than 'read'. By reading a more intellectually challenging book than you would usually, you would be able to push yourself and exercise your brain as much as you are exercising your body. You could increase your vocabulary with authors who can liberate you in their use of the English language, from the mundane to the sublime. If you did, then you would be proactively managing your resilience at the same time.

- **So, think of a word and add an exclamation mark to it! We have explored two examples, but maybe you could try others and become 'creative!' rather than 'creative'.**

Over time, you will be more in control of your resilience by proactively giving yourself a balance of experiences. Who knows, after a few months you may well feel like a superhero about your achievements. 'WOW!'

9. LOTIONS. POTIONS AND SOLUTIONS

Visit the Mind Shop as well as the Body Shop

- Clue 1 – What company started in Brighton in 1976 and, according to its own website, has been *rule breaking, never faking and change making* ever since?

- Clue 2 – The founder of this business proactively supported projects on human rights, environmental issues and animal protection across the world.

- Clue 3 – Sometimes directly attacking the ethics of her own industry, the Dame who founded this brand of shops, promoted (and was known for) cosmetic products that are not tested on animals.

- Clue 4 – She was also known for her direct opposition to the stereotyping of women and 'skinny models' and they do not appear in the adverts for her body products.

Now in 26 countries around the world, Anita Roddick's Body Shop brand has come a long way away from its original base. Although Roddick passed away in 2007, the company maintains a keenness, over 40 years after its founding, to *enhance people's natural beauty across the globe*. But what if there was a new range of products – a collection of lotions, potions and solutions that would cleanse and enhance not the body, but the mind? Rather than the Body Shop, it could be called the Mind Shop, with shelves stacked with products that purported to improve your mental well-being and happiness.

LIFT!

'SLEEP SALVE'

Not to be taken with caffeine or alcohol.
No internet, TV or mobile devices an hour before use.

'ALLEVIATING AIR'

Best administered outdoors and in naturally occurring surroundings, such as woodland or parks.

'PAUSE PATCHES'

Side-effects could include a clearer solution to the problem area.
Proven to help reduce irrational responses to situations of all kinds.

'INTEGRITY INFUSION'

Allows the true You to emerge.
Originates with authenticity.

- **Maybe you could be creative and think of some more products for the Mind Shop?**

Sleep, as you know, does not need a salve, but does need a solution. You, like others, need your 'beauty sleep' as it is vital for your body to recharge itself and organise your thinking. Your mind, while at rest, can help to sort out the twists and tangles of the day.

Similarly, fresh air can alleviate many of your woes, just as the packaging for 'Alleviating Air' suggests. Walk along the promenade at the seaside and soon the waves and salty, sea air will invigorate you. Even a simple walk can stretch out your legs but can also exercise your mind too – a win/win situation.

'Pause Patches', if they somehow were able to alert you to stop every now and again, would surely be a bestseller. Or, are you able to convince yourself that you haven't got long enough to stop? Actually, if you are thinking that, then it is probably the perfect time to stop.

But do you also need an 'Integrity Infusion'? There will inevitably be times when you may have to compromise your integrity to a degree, but maybe more resilient souls will ensure that they retain it more often?

I do not think for one minute that the Body Shop will expand its range of lotions, potions and solutions to include my suggested new products. However, I do believe that taking time to consider the needs of your mind as much as your body is beneficial. The good news is you don't need a product range to achieve this; it comes free of charge. Rather, it is just a change in mindset and an investment in your inner self that is required.

10. HOOKING UP A HOSE

How a strong connection is crucial to the flow of ideas

Water is crucial in the production of crops, and throughout history we have tried to combat the laws of nature to find ways of growing food in a wider range of locations than previously thought possible. However, with the demand for food continuing to rise, humans still have to consider ever-more inventive ways to irrigate the land. The shaduf, the Archimedes' Screw and rain seeding have been three crucial developments

- **The shaduf is a simple lever system that follows the principles of a playground see-saw. In short, a stone (called the counterweight) is attached to one end of a pivot and then a bucket on to the other. Controlled by a single person, the newly lifted water can be tipped into a series of channels that subsequently soak the land. Used widely in India and Egypt to this day, this primitive yet effective method allows farmers to irrigate their crops.**

- The Archimedes' Screw, named after the well-known Greek thinker, is a device to raise water from a river to flood the crops. Through a manual twisting on the screw, the water is drawn up and held against the inner surface of the casing by gravity. Greeks, Romans and Egyptians all used a variant of this invention, but the principle remained the same and is still effective for localised flooding of the land.

- Rain seeding is a more modern method to irrigate the land. This process requires firing silver iodide into the air, which then induces condensation and forms a rain cloud. The water droplets condense and fall as rain. If you search for the 'Thailand Royal Rainmaking Project', 'Beijing Olympics rain' or 'Russian military parade rain' then you'll see that this is a worldwide phenomenon.

Whichever form of irrigation is used, crops of rice, wheat and corn (maize) still dominate global use of water. In fact, two-thirds of total water consumption is taken up by these three cereal crops alone. The watering of the crops creates the food (which contains the water) that we need. Indeed, the proportion of an average adult human is also around 60 per cent water, depending on your size and shape; put simply, we are mostly water! In fact, our brains, muscles and hearts are 73 per cent, 83 per cent and 78 per cent water, respectively.

You already know that good hydration leads to greater efficiency and improved productivity. However, getting your eight glasses of water, despite knowing that you need them, is hard to achieve. You have no doubt felt the effects that even slight dehydration can have on your levels of tiredness, energy and therefore work rate. Any drop in productivity inevitably leads to needing longer to complete any given task. Continue in this way for any length of time and there will be a negative effect on your ability to 'keep up', leading to a fall in composure and a rise in stress levels.

Scientific evidence suggests that even a 1 to 3 per cent drop in hydration levels can lead to:

- **fatigue;**

- **impaired memory;**

- **headaches;**

- **reduced cognitive performance.**

These effects (as well as many others) clearly make you less resilient in rising to the challenges of your daily tasks. The workplace is already pressurised enough. You don't need to inadvertently do anything to exacerbate this.

- Take some time now to reflect upon how proactive you are at managing your hydration. You have read about various ways to irrigate land, but how can you rise to the challenge of meeting your own personal hydration needs?

II. THE RUBRIC OF RUBIK 💡

How a methodical approach can solve seemingly complex problems

- **If you were asked to think back to childhood games where colour was a dominant feature, what comes into your mind? Twister or Rubik's Cube?**

If it was Twister, then there were four circles of each of the four primary colours. The giant spinner (well, it seemed giant at the time) demanded 'right foot on yellow', 'left hand on green'. The randomised element to the game was the mechanism where everyone ended up contorted and intertwined until someone fell over.

In 1976, the Rubik's Cube was first produced. This may be surprising as it is often classed as an icon of the 1980s. The cube had six sides, each made up of nine smaller squares on each face. Again, it shared the same colours as Twister with yellow, green, blue and red, but what were the fifth and sixth colours? Those of you who took the stickers off in an attempt to 'solve' the cube would know that they were white and orange.

Pre-internet, children who were keen to solve the cube turned to a 13 year-old, Patrick Bossert, and his book *You Can Do the Cube*. This teenager's algorithm has now been superseded, but at the time gave you the best chance of impressing your friends and family with a completed coloured cube.

If you are faced with a Twister-scale problem in real life, consider ways to disentangle yourself from the knot that you are in. Asked to perform one more action, you need to think through where best to move in order to create a more stable overall position. Careful and considerate placement will allow you to get more of a foothold on the problem that you are facing. Gradually, this will build confidence that, in turn, will allow you to improve your overall performance with other tasks.

Alternatively, you may feel overstretched with the level of responsibility that you have been given. This can have a negative effect on your resilience as your confidence levels drop, leaving you feeling that you cannot do the task that has been asked of you. Also, you can ask for guidance from others who can offer a new perspective and can let you know what the best next move is.

If on the other hand you are faced with a Rubik's Cube-scale problem in real life, consider how best to break the problem down into easier manageable steps. All too often the problem as a whole appears too big, too cumbersome to be achievable. However, by tackling the problem bit by bit you can get closer to the overall solution. By first getting the yellow side done, you could then start on the greens. Cumulatively, these add up to something much bigger, meaning you can achieve the whole of the challenge that you previously considered impossible!

Overall, whether it is a 'cube-sized' problem, or an 'in a twist' issue, you can do something about it, however complex it first appears. Careful consideration as to the first and then the best next move will allow you to untangle yourself or to be able to combine smaller, bite-sized components into an overall solution. To achieve this, you will need to draw on your inner resilience, and finding a solution will inevitably boost your future resilience too.

12. PARKING PARAMETERS ⏸

At times you feel like you can't stop – but you can

- **If you were to guess the constituent parts that make up road-marking paint, what would you say they were?**

Classed as thermoplastic paint, or hot-melt parking paint, its name gives you a clue to its main component, plastic. When subjected to heat (thermo–) it melts to form a hard-wearing, brightly coloured strip of colour that determines the parking restrictions for a particular piece of road.

- **Would you have expected the second ingredient to be lead?**

Yellow lead, or lead chromate, is still used for colouring the single and double yellow lines on our roads, despite the fact that lead has been classed as hazardous since the nineteenth century. It remains an exception to the rules as engineers and scientists explore viable, more environmentally friendly and safer alternatives to give the markings their distinctive and well-known colouration.

- **Would you have expected the third ingredient to be glass?**

It is the reflective qualities of glass that make it perfect for safety-conscious councils who are looking to make the lines even clearer in the dark. In a technology similar to the cat's-eyes that run down the central lines on some of our roads, the glass particles within the thermoplastic strip reflect the beams from car headlights. Shaped in a very particular way, they make the markings clearer for motorists and thus potentially reduce road traffic accidents.

Since 1996, new drivers have had to take a theory test as well as a practical driving test. One element of the exam is about the rules of road markings, ie knowing the law governing single and double yellow lines on the road and kerb. For example, vertical yellow markings on a kerbstone mean 'No loading or unloading at the times shown on the nearby sign'.

Now that you have refreshed your Highway Code knowledge about parking, stopping and unloading, consider what your Personal Code might be in terms of allowing you to stop and take stock.

- **Do you know when you personally are allowed to halt in everyday life and in your job?**

- **Are you aware of your own yellow line markings – when shouldn't you stop?**

- **When do you stop and unload, safe in the knowledge that it is OK to do so?**

Importantly, stopping can give you time to think more clearly and allows you the opportunity to re-evaluate. It can bring you back to the present moment, so that rather than focusing on what has previously happened, or what might happen, you can consider what is happening now. Put a different way, rather than driving frantically towards a dead end, you might be better placed to return to the junction and turn a different way. If you do not allow yourself a pause for thought then you restrict your ability to think with clarity or to draw on the associated benefits.

Similarly, you know that sharing the load is beneficial whether that load is a workload or an emotional load. Either way, there are times you need to share that load out so that you feel that it is possible to deal with the challenge facing you. A characteristic of resilience is, after all, to feel in control and empowered rather than overwrought.

Just like the glass in the thermoplastic strips is a safety upgrade that allows us to see more clearly, I hope this chapter also allows you to see with greater clarity the importance of stopping, rethinking or unloading. Pausing for a breath and giving yourself the time to consider your options is crucial for your resilience and well-being.

13. PIXELATED PICTURES 👁

How zooming out of Hanjie puzzles gives you the full picture

Here are two grids.

9	1			2	5	8		
						1	9	5
		6		3				
1	6				8		5	
		8				4		1
	9		1	7	3			
3			8					
5			3			2	4	
	8	2		9				

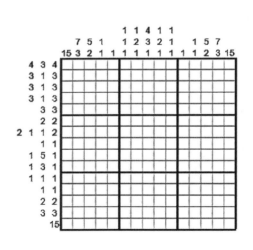

The grid on the left contains nine 3 × 3 squares. It is a Sudoku puzzle that requires you to fill the grid so that each square, line and column contains the numbers one to nine only once. There are starter numbers to get you underway. Despite being commonly thought of as Japanese in origin, Sudoku was a renaming of an American puzzle called 'Number Place'.

The grid on the right contains nine 5 × 5 squares. It is a Hanjie puzzle that requires you to fill the grid so that each square is coloured according to the numbers that run along the top and left-hand side of the grid. This brain-teaser, despite being a Japanese puzzle, has now been renamed by *Daily Telegraph* readers as the rather American-sounding 'Griddler'.

However, regardless of their origin, each puzzle has evolved from being unknown to being found in publications on a daily basis. Indeed, it was the exponential growth in the popularity of Sudoku that led people to look for the next Sudoku-like puzzle. This gave rise to the publication of Hanjie, especially for those looking for an alternative number-placement challenge. The Japanese graphics editor, Non Ishida, who created the first Hanjie puzzle started to spot pictures within the patterns that are created by skyscrapers' lights being either on or off in the various windows – and thus a new puzzle was born.

What is fascinating about Hanjie puzzles is the fact that, on initial sight, they appear to be random sequences of numbers and yet, once completed and combined, they create a recognisable image of something. Close up, these puzzles retain their blocky, almost child-like image quality. It is only when you zoom out, that you begin to see a fuller, more complete picture. Similarly, seen close up, the pattern of lights in the various windows of the skyscraper would be difficult to interpret. You need to see them from a distance to get a clearer overall appearance.

Comparably, when you are too close to a problem, you can't see the full picture. This can make you start to doubt yourself, your confidence drops and your resilience follows in the same downwards direction. You can see some of the elements that make up that picture, but the 'global overview' can allude you. So step back from the situation and reflect on what you are looking at – what part do you have to play within the team? What is your role in the greater scheme of things?

If you are not able to do this yourself then ask others to help you. If you are locked into a state where you can't see whether the 1 or the 9 go into a particular Sudoku square, then you need someone to have a fresh look at the situation and to help you to make that call. If you don't know whether to shade this square, or that square, it might take someone else to work it out for you. In a similar way, when you can't see the way forwards, you need someone to offer their perspective on whatever it is that is bothering you.

14. INFINITY AND BEYOND ⓫

∞ *If you are making continuous loops, you need to stop and pause*

- **Which three numbers, when rotated 90 degrees, make well-known mathematical symbols?**

The numbers 1, 11 and 8 make -, = and ∞, respectively.

The 'rotated-eight' symbol, the infinity sign, still fascinates mathematicians as they grapple with the continuum of numbers. Möbius, a nineteenth-century German mathematician and astronomer, who had an interest in the limitless possibilities of both disciplines, supposedly developed the now infamous sign while considering these infinite concepts. He created a 3D version of the symbol that can be made very easily from a strip of paper. Cut a thin strip from the long side of a piece of A4 paper. Secure the ends of this strip together with glue but also add the all-important single twist before you do so to create the 'figure of eight' effect.

LIFT!

Now add a border to this shape – a continuous line that runs along its length. With a black pen, start at any point and work your way along that edge until you return to where you started. It was this effect that inspired artist M C Escher to make his 'Möbius I' and 'Möbius II' woodcuts in the 1960s.

With a new strip of paper, create another Möbius Strip but first time write the months of the year on it to form a 'timeline'. Write the first six months along the bottom edge of the front side of the strip (ideally equally spaced along it). Then flip the strip over (horizontally) and write all the months July to December on the reverse side (again on the bottom edge). Now create that same paper twist, before securing the ends together. You should have created a continuous 'loop of time'.

This is like your academic year – as each year passes, you return to the same month and you lap again, albeit with different children in your classes, or your school. You travel around and through the 'Möbius Timeline' of your school calendar until you reach the beginning again. In many ways this is a positive thing as it creates known entities and a clear routine. However, it also brings with it a truism that can sometimes be forgotten.

Regardless of how quickly you complete your lap, you will get there nonetheless. Like a Grand Prix, you drive round your circuits (sometimes at break-neck speed) only to come back to the same point. Yes, you might win a race if you were a Formula One driver, but most of us aren't. You need to mitigate the urge to go at an unwise pace and instead seek opportunities to regulate your speed – and maybe even enjoy the view along the way! By creating something that is more sustainable, you will be able to keep going for longer (and crucially with less likelihood of damaging yourself in the process).

- **As you consider the loop of your academic year, reflect on how best to pace yourself, take pit-stops and breaks to allow yourself to 'refuel'.**

You will become increasingly aware of the benefits that come with doing this: increased productivity, more alertness and a greater keenness than previously thought. This is not an optical illusion like a Möbius Strip; this is a reality that will help you survive your year.

15. OH. HOW THE CHOCOLATE FLOWS

Top yourself up to have enough to go around

- **What are Forastero, Criollo and Trinitario?**

They are the three most common cocoa beans that are used to make our beloved chocolate. The versatile Forastero, grown in countries such as Ecuador and Brazil, is the least susceptible to disease and thus has a 90 per cent share of the market. The other 10 per cent of the market is shared between Trinitario and the lesser known pods of Criollo.

Once picked, these pods open to reveal the cocoa beans, which are left out to dry in the tropical sun. These dried beans are shipped to countries that will roast, grind and blend the beans to make the final bar. The ground-up cocoa beans get combined with the other ingredients of sugar, milk, vegetable oils and vanilla flavourings to suit the requirements of that particular country.

Due to its high sugar content, chocolate is heat-sensitive, which is crucial to know if you are going to use it in a chocolate fountain. This showpiece needs the chocolate to be warmed gently in order to flow evenly over its multi-layered tiers. Depending on the proportions of other ingredients that have been added, the heat required to make the fountain flow will change accordingly.

However, regardless of whether you get the heat right, the fountain will only work if there is enough chocolate in the system. The host will need to top it up as quickly as the guests are indulging. If they don't then the fountain will stop flowing over the levels and will eventually run dry. Should this happen then it will take considerable effort to get it going again, or it will burn out entirely.

In a similar way, your energy levels are not unlimited. If you keep giving or other people keep taking from you then you will also run dry. If you do not top yourself up, then your multi-layered tiers will not have anything flowing over them. This is not a prescription for chocolate consumption but rather an analogy to encourage you to top yourself up in whatever way you think is best. This could be watching a movie, going out for a meal or taking a walk in the park with the dog. Whatever it is, you need to self-regulate frequently!

The average chocolate consumption in Britain is currently three bars a week; you may be 'above expected', 'as expected' or 'below expected' according to this threshold figure. But, while chocolate may be comfort food, perhaps you could find three alternative ways to top yourself up? You could directly address this need by allowing yourself to have some 'me time'. This could be times in the week where you read a book, have a candle-lit bath or watch that box set.

The Forastero is the most popular bean as it is less susceptible to disease. Milk chocolate is preferred for chocolate fountains, as this is less susceptible to heat. What combination of techniques could you employ to make you less susceptible to burnout? If you consider your average weekly or even daily routines, would you say that you have got enough time within them to allow you to top yourself up? Chocolate feels decadent and is a treat. You need to consider other treats that you can give yourself that allow you to nurture your overall energy levels and to build your resilience.

16. SCOTOMA – WE'VE ALL GOT ONE 👁

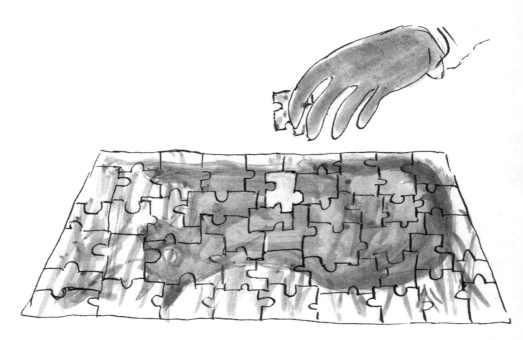

Overcome your blind spots, even though they are still there

- **What can you remember from school science lessons about rods, cones and retinas?**

The term retina relates to the surface at the back of the eye. Like a camera, light enters the eye (regulated by the iris) and, with the help of a lens, projects an inverted copy of the image onto the retina. This retinal surface is full of light-receptive cells called rods and cones. Rods receive information from low-level light, while cones do the same from brighter light. The proportion of rods and cones differs from species to species and this determines their ability to see effectively in the dark. For example, an Australian bird called the tawny frogmouth has got superb night-vision due to the number of rod receptor cells it has.

Together, rods and cones create a complete or nearly complete version of what you are currently looking at. It is only nearly complete because, as well as being upside-down, each image has a blurred oval in it. This oval, created by a biological fault, is called a blind spot. You have one – you just don't see it. In reality, you do see the blind spot all the time; it is just that your brain is able to 'fill in' the space.

Called *scotoma* in medical circles, this fault is something that humans have been able to overcome thanks to some clever adaptations. This missing area of vision is interpolated with the colours of the objects from either the surrounding environment or with information from previous images that the eye has already captured.

In a similar way, you also have blind spots in real life – places where you don't really see the full picture. Just like the brain interpolating to cover up any scotoma, you need to seek ways to fill in the gaps in your perception or to check what you have missed. This blind spot can either be something that is known about yet ignored; or it can be something that is not known about, and therefore you cannot do anything other than ignore it. Conscious awareness of the issue can raise its profile and allow you to reflect, consider and subsequently plan to mitigate against it.

In the first instance, it is sometimes best to face up to a problem rather than spend time worrying about what might happen or dwelling on worst-case scenarios that may never come to pass. Ignoring something that you know about doesn't make the situation any better. Like the young child who puts their hands over their eyes and thinks that you can't see them, this is not an accurate perception; you are kidding yourself. You would be wise to stop ignoring it and dip into your inner reserves of resilience, admit that it is there and start to address it.

Alternatively, if the blind spot is formed due to a gap in your experience then this is much harder to allay. This is why resilience is no longer classed as an individual pursuit – you need the vision of different people to reaffirm the complete image. Asking more experienced colleagues for support through constructive feedback can sometimes help. Honest advice followed by rational self-reflection can often lead to positive solutions to problems. Together, you will be able to address your scotoma.

17. SHAKEN, YET UNDETERRED ⏱

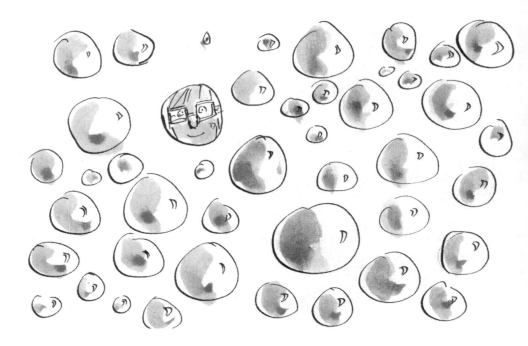

Gradually dissipate the inevitable fizz in your life

The crown cork, the bottle-top commonly called a beer bottle-top, was patented by William Painter in 1892. Its 'teeth' clasp the top of the bottle while a cork seal prevents any contact between the contents and the metal cap. To open these bottles, a bottle opener is used to bend back the teeth before pouring the contents into a glass. A century later, the artist Molly B Right used thousands of crown cap bottle-tops to create her portraits of famous figures such as Gandhi, Einstein and Queen Elizabeth II.

In a similar fashion, it took around 180,000 ring pulls from drinks cans for the artist Herman Divers to create a full-sized replica of a 'Harley Davison' motorcycle. What would Ermal Fraze, who invented this infamous can-opening method, make of Divers' classic car and motorbike sculptures? Fraze's integrated opening system, patented in 1959, removed the need for a bottle opener and therefore was more practical when out and about.

Plastic bottles were first used commercially in 1947 but remained expensive until the 1950s when 'high-density polyethylene' (a strong plastic) was able to create the well-known screw top lid. This most practical of inventions is also used to create an artwork about the importance of recycling. The sculpture, by Mary Ellen Croteau, is an eight by seven feet self-portrait made from more than 7,000 of these plastic bottle caps.

All three types of lid are able to keep the millions of carbon dioxide molecules within the container until the consumer wants to release them, with that familiar psshhhhhhh sound. Pending the crown cap release, the ring pull draw back, or the plastic top rotation, the contents are virtually 'bubble-free', it's only the release of the pressure on opening that create them.

Similarly, you are also a vessel that is under pressure. It is almost a natural by-product of modern life; your internal pressure increases over time. Allowed to build up unaddressed, you risk a mini-explosion. Your daily life does more than shake you up, so you need to do something to dissipate this regularly and proactively (while still retaining some inner fizz too). Whereas the ring pull and crown cap are an either/or, open/closed option, the screw cap allows for that graduated approach. One twist can dissipate the first bit of the pressure, the second twist, a little more. This form of regulation is much more beneficial to you.

Resilience is not the removal of fizz, or the total absence of fizz. Just like the bottle or can, you contain bubbles too. Lurking and ever-present, you need to remain shaken, yet undeterred. You know they are there, you just need to do more to address them. You must try to acknowledge when you are under pressure and do more to proactively release the fizz along the way. What can you do to achieve this screw-top twist?

- **You need to be consciously aware that there is a build-up and learn to recognise your own signs and symptoms of when this is happening. All too often you can kid yourself that you are OK; on the surface you appear calm and yet underneath, you are bubbling. Not wanting to be that person who is not coping, you battle on in the hope that it will dissipate. However, this is rarely the case and you need to do more; otherwise you will inevitably go pop!**

- **You need to release a few of these bubbles frequently by spending just a few minutes where you focus on your breathing, perform some creative visualisation or simply go outside into the fresh air. These quick, simple actions will help to relax you, reassure you and boost your resilience before you re-embark on the task in hand.**

Useful websites

www.mollybright.com
www.grassrootsart.net/art/HermanDivers.html
www.maryellencroteau.net

18. TEA: THE DRINK, OR WHO WE DRINK WITH?

Sharing a cuppa can teach you the benefits of pausing

- **Square, round or pyramid?**

These are the questions that advertising executives have challenged shoppers with since loose leaf tea was first encapsulated within a filter bag. Since the 1960s, when tea was 'square', it took nearly 30 years for them to move towards the circle-shaped teabag. With its trimmed edges, arguably there was less 'brew-room' for the tea. Indeed, it was clear that the quality of contents outweighed the shape of the bag when it came to our nation's favourite beverage. Soon after, consumers were offered pyramid-shapes in an attempt to increase the 'brew-space'. But it is the familiarity of the process of making the brew that is key to our enjoyment of the drink, rather than the bag being square, round or pyramidal.

- **All of which is a 'storm in a tea cup', isn't it?**

Whether it's English Breakfast or Earl Grey or the wonderful-sounding Lapsang Souchong, they all start out from the plant, Camellia Sinensis. Essentially, they are a blend of leaves grown in different climatic regions across the globe with the possible addition of an extra element to make each unique.

Take English Breakfast tea as an example. This is a blend of black teas originating from India, Sri Lanka and Kenya. It was popularised by Queen Victoria after a trip to Balmoral where she tasted the then 'breakfast tea' blend and brought it back to England where she coined the preceding word of 'English'. Similarly, Earl Grey has a connection with the prime minister of the time. In the 1830s, this black tea mix had the additional element of bergamot (orange) oil added to it for that noticeable twang. Alternatively, to give Lapsang Souchong tea its unmistakable flavour, the leaves are placed in bamboo baskets and smoked over smouldering pinewood fires.

- **Which of the three is your cup of tea?**

Whether it's milk first, then the tea; to squeeze the tea bag or not; or to warm the teapot first with boiling water, we all have rituals and processes that surround the making of this quintessentially English drink. Indeed, it is the ritual of sitting and sharing time together over a 'cuppa' that makes it the nation's favourite. Time to catch up, share news and enjoy each other's company, tea offers us the excuse to pause, reflect and exchange. For this reason, it remains an important cohesion mechanism, providing the socially accepted code for building connections with others.

Possibly, this is the reason that teabags still come connected in pairs? Tea for two; the tea bag reminding us that we need to invite another to come and share the experience with us.

Like tea-drinking, resilience is not a lone pursuit. You have the inbuilt need to connect with others and tea (or indeed coffee) is one way that you can achieve this. So, invite your biggest supporter to share an English Breakfast with you – that person who will boost your confidence with their unreserved, unconditional celebration of who you are. Share an Earl Grey with the person who will switch you off from work and be able to talk about other things. Or, try a Lapsang Souchong with a colleague of yours who will be willing and able to constructively challenge you and help to recalibrate yourself with their valued opinion.

- **Whoever it is, ask 'Anyone for a brew?'**

19. LORRY LIMITS ⏱

Learn your limits and let others know what they are

- **What's the connection between a common toad and a yellow vulture?**

The first speed limit on British roads was introduced in 1865. At the time, this limited cars from travelling no more than four miles an hour. Some 38 years later, in 1903, this had risen to 20 mph, and then again to 30 mph in 1935; a law that is still in place to this day in built-up areas. By 1965, the enforcement on motorways began with a separate 70 mph speed limit being imposed – a law that drivers know about and mostly adhere to.

Not long after the first increase in the speed limit, around 1908, Kenneth Grahame published the *The Wind in the Willows*. Is there is a connection between the speeding character in his book and the new laws regarding speed? Mr Toad, a 'common toad', may well have been a way to teach children, and the adults who read the stories to them, about these new speed restrictions.

With the protection of air bags, APS brakes and advanced safety belt features, drivers are being falsely numbed to the speed that they are travelling. However, newer, more innovative methods are now in place to challenge this common misperception. One such measure is the introduction of Smart Motorways and the Average Speed Camera systems that are becoming increasingly prevalent. From the first fixed speed cameras, introduced in 1999, technology has progressed significantly. Indeed, these 'yellow vultures' – the nickname given to these cameras – can simultaneously recognise your number plate as well as start an internal timer. When you pass the second camera, further down the road, the computer can calculate your speed over time by re-matching your number plate and concurrently stopping the timer.

So, the connection between a common toad and a yellow vulture is that they are both to do with speed regulation – the need to know your limits and to not exceed them. The idea of an average speed can also act as a pacemaker; a way of regulating yourself and moderating your behaviour when you are in danger of exceeding your limitations. Modern life is so hectic, as you try to fit more and more into your days, that you can easily reach the point where you are over-running yourself and need to take stock.

Protected by the effects of adrenaline, caffeine and sheer willpower, you are likely to be regularly exceeding your limits. You avoid the signs and proceed on with rugged determination, suppressing the feeling with a little glass of something. And yet, what you need to do is to pull over and visit a service station. You should allow yourself a pit stop every now and again to refuel.

- **Do you think that you are a 30 mph or 70 mph person?**
- **Is 30 mph where you think you should be?**
- **Is the reality that 70 mph is your term-time speed and 4 mph is your holiday speed?**

You are the person who knows your limits better than anyone else. Nevertheless, just like the invention of Smart Motorways, you need to be smarter too. You need to find a more sustainable speed (maybe 50 mph) for yourself in order to maintain your resilience. If you don't, then you are going to get caught out, just like Mr Toad! So instead, be smart and regulate your speed as you go about your day.

20. STRIKE A CHORD

Consider what you want to convey, but also how you convey yourself

Sounding more like enemies of Doctor Who, dyads, triads and tetrads are actually groups of notes that, when played together, make a chord. Imagine that you are sitting at a piano and you press down one of the white keys, to play a single note. Now play that note at the same time as the white key four to the right of it. Played together, these notes form a dyad – a simple two-note chord.

In a similar way, three notes that 'agree with each other' are called triads. These form slightly more complex chords using every other white key. Whatever your starting point, putting your fingers on keys number one, three and five creates a harmonious chord.

In jazz or blues music, they tend to use tetrad chords – or combinations of four notes that play well together. This is the starting note (the first) as before, played with the third, fifth and seventh notes concurrently. Art Tatum, one of the most virtuosic pianists in the history of jazz, included tetrads in his songs. Be warned, if you watch a video of him, his hands are so fast across the keys that you'll be lucky to see his fingers in the tetrad positions. When all the notes work well together then this is described as a 'concord'. However, if a less-experienced musician is at the keyboard then it may be described as a 'discord', with each note jarring with the other.

Just as individual notes belong to a wider group of notes, you as an individual need to offer your own unique contribution when part of a group of two, three, four, or more. As part of a group you can celebrate your differences, play to your strengths and use your unique abilities so that together you can aspire to being something more symphonic.

With active effort and practice, you can train yourself to concentrate on not only the things that you have in common with the people around you, but also on those things that set you slightly apart. You have similar emotions, similar values, similar insecurities and similar vulnerabilities. However, you are a better person if you work together with others; even if there is discord at times.

When connecting to others, you need to resonate or create a concord with those around you. It is only when you do that true connection can occur and that a trust relationship can develop. You have a deep-seated need to connect with others. You also benefit in terms of your own resilience when you get it right – when you strike a chord with someone else, together you can boost each other.

If you have developed this trust relationship with the person over time, then they will be more likely to hear and respond positively to any feedback that you might give them. Then when there is the inevitable discord between you, or a difficult conversation that needs to be had, you are both more likely to frame what needs to be said in a way that is more empathetic and meaningful. You will give/receive more balanced points of view that seek to provoke discussion and remain truthful, but will be more easily absorbed by the giver/receiver. In short, we need to connect with the person before we are in the position to correct them.

However, these are skills that need to be practised over time, and my suggestion would be to start today. Try to develop your skills in order to do battle with your dyads, triads and tetrads, like a Doctor Who.

21. IS YOUR TEACHING SPARKLING OR FLAT?

Get the autonomy you need to make your teaching sparkle

- **'Do you want water with that, madam? Sparkling or still?'**

Many of us would say 'Just some tap water, please'. But what exactly is the difference between sparkling mineral water and tap water? What are you paying the extra money for?

In order to answer this question, you need to remind yourself of the chemistry lessons that you may have had when you were at secondary school. The periodic table attempted to organise all the known elements in the world onto one chart. Currently, scientists claim to know 118 of these basic building blocks.

Placed into columns and rows (called periods), the elements are lined up according to their protons, neutrons and electrons. Most elements have one or two letters as their chemical symbols - a capital

LIFT!

letter followed by a lower-case letter. For example, He is helium. However, some of the newer elements that scientists have uncovered have three letters, like ununpentium: Uup

So, let's try a few to see if you can recall this knowledge...

- **Ca is the chemical symbol for which element?**
- **What about Mg? (Clue: this element does include these letters within its name.)**
- **What element is represented by the letter K?**
- **Na is the symbol for which element on the periodic table?**

Answers: Ca is Calcium, Mg is Magnesium, K is Potassium, Na is Sodium. (To note, K is for Kalium and Na is for Natrium; both are their Latin names.)

Why are we interested in these four elements? Well, located on the far left of the Periodic Table, these are the four main minerals that are found in bottled water. It is the proportion of these elements that make up its distinctive taste. If you add CO_2 as well then you have your sparkling water.

- **But how does that relate to your teaching?**
- **What is 'sparkling' teaching?**
- **How does that differ from 'flat' teaching?**
- **How do you add the bubbles of CO_2 to make you effervescent in front of your pupils?**

I believe that the 'C' in CO_2 should be Choice and the 'O' is Options. It is autonomy – the feeling that you have some choice in both *what* you teach and also *how* you teach it – that is a key motivator. Additionally, having options gives you the lift that is needed to drive you onwards and help you feel in control of what you are doing. This, at some small yet important level, is empowerment – a key element of resilience.

If empowerment can lead to engagement, then this in turn can resonate with your learners. If you tune into your pupils' needs, then they will respond enthusiastically and this reflects back to you. In this way, a positive feedback mechanism is established that stems from the introduction of choice. It sounds so simple and yet, at the same time, it is so effective when you get it right.

So, in summary, if given the choice, then take that choice. When given options, explore those options. And combining them gives you the CO_2 to make the bubbles that you need to make you sparkle! Collating them will keep you motivated; connecting them will allow you to feel empowered. Altogether this builds up your resilience as well as the resilience of others in your care. What are you going to choose now, sparkling, or still?

22. BINARY BARCODES 👁

You sometimes see things as a one or a zero, but is this accurate?

You'd be forgiven for thinking that the barcode world was simply one that is black or white, but that would be like saying that all zebras are the same. Just as a zebra's stripes come in all different patterns, unique to each individual, barcodes do too. They are unique, with each digit represented by a pattern of black and white stripes.

More importantly, however, each digit of a barcode is symbolised by exactly seven stripes. Each of these stripes is either black or white. The next digit is also seven stripes but will be a different combination unique to that number. By standardising the pattern for each digit, all companies can correlate that barcode sequence to a specific product, factory or publisher, anywhere in the world!

Take the number 3 for example. This is an alternating white, black, white, black sequence of '1-4-1-1'.

Whereas the number 6 is '1-1-1-4'.

Rather than the classic black and white stripes of a barcode, newspapers used to employ a technique called 'halftone' that used the size of individual dots to convey apparent lightness and darkness.

Halftone colouring helps to convey more detail in a picture but it is an illusion that is easily spotted when you get closer to the picture. Taking it further, modern computer screens can display 256 distinct gradations of the colour grey that range from pure black to pure white.

So, rather than considering everyday issues as black or white barcode-like situations, start to look at them as halftone gradations, or shades of grey instead. Moving gradually between gradations can feel less restricted and constrained. This somewhat smoother transition can also give you more options and therefore a sense of control. It can facilitate an easier transition between where you are now and where you need to get to.

In reality, the human eye can distinguish around 30 greys and that should be ample for most situations. These small steps make them feel even more achievable. Each one can be completed with less effort and in less time. It can also feel less overwhelming, more reasonable and more realistic to achieve.

- **Consider your current problem from a barcode, halftone or computer monitor viewpoint and decide for yourself which perspective makes the problem feel easier to tackle.**

Sometimes you may feel that you are without choices, but the reality is that there are a number of different options available to you at any given time. Your perception may be that the only step available is a 'giant step' from black to white. In truth, this is not so. A more accurate position is available if you give yourself the time to stop and consider the problem, the context and then, hopefully, the graded path to the solution. Time allows you the luxury to explore these, but you rarely allow yourself, or are given by others, these vital minutes of reflection and contemplation.

- **Are you making that decision for yourself or others?**
- **What factors are impacting your decision?**
- **Is your perception based in fact or fiction?**
- **Are you judging yourself and the situation rationally?**
- **Can you draw on family, friends or colleagues to affirm the steps of your journey?**

By answering these questions, you will remind yourself of the choices that you have. In short, choice is empowering, autonomy is a great motivator and you always have choices; as long as you take the time to notice that you have them. By knowing this, it will boost your resilience and give you the confidence to proceed on your journey.

23. HENRY'S PAIL 💡

You can be more effective if you fix the hole in your bucket

- **What would you be building if you were to select an aquifer, an auger and an ampule as your 'A-list'?**

Any well needs to draw its water from somewhere. This water 'sits' within the bedrock, deep underground. If you commission a survey, then they will scan the chosen location until they find the aquifer – there's the water. To access this water, you will need to drill down using a specialist piece of equipment called an auger, which is capable of extruding that amount of soil – there's the access to that water. All you need to do now is to send a bucket down to 'fetch the pail of water' – you could do this using an ampule.

But, what if that bucket had a hole in it? That was the question that Henry faced in the famous song – the boy who was helped by dear Liza. The advice to mend the bucket with straw refers to a past when buckets were made from wood and looked more like half-barrels than buckets. The short planks of wood, called staves, were held together with 'hoops' made from either flexible pieces of wood (called withies); if not, then with galvanised iron strips.

In actual fact, although still a temporary solution, both straw and wood do swell when wet and therefore a small hole could be effectively sealed until a more substantial repair could be done. However, the original problem would remain and thus would still need to be properly fixed by a cooper – he could certainly put the bucket together again. In fact, if Humpty no longer needed his wall, the bricks would make a lovely surround for your new well!

Rather than turning to straw to patch up the holes in your 'buckets', you need to seek out and find the 'cooperage solutions' to problems. Try to avoid temporary fixes. You need to identify the root of the problem and do something directly to address the issue head-on. Rather than swerving or ignoring that 'niggling doubt', you need to either deal with it yourself or find someone who can help you. An hour spent on resolution is five times that saved in the future. You need to see it as 'paying forwards', an investment that will reap dividends further down the line.

Your desire to become more efficient and effective in the long term is hampered by your yearning to not waste any time in the short term. With 'time' being such a precious commodity, you may be tempted by faster yet temporary fixes in an attempt to get today's tasks completed. You might be lured with the 'quick wins' rather than properly fixing the 'leaky bucket'. But this will affect your resilience. This inefficiency gradually chips away at your confidence and self-esteem. Over time, this can have a significant and detrimental effect.

A resilient teacher looks to the longer-term solution rather than transitional gains. This approach needs you to have a vision for the future but also requires that time is spent considering and planning the steps needed to be taken in order to achieve that vision. In your busy daily schedule, you do not usually have that moment for reflection and so there needs to be a considered, direct allocation of your time to make it happen. Given its importance, you would be wise to at least consider putting it into your daily, weekly or monthly timetable. This could then act as a prompt or reminder to consider where the leaks in your buckets are, and then access and allocate the resources to fix them.

24. THE HOLE IN THE WALL ⏸

Manage the amount you draw out of your account

- **Are you a repeater, a sequencer or a dater?**

They sound like a crew of robbers about to take on a heist, don't they? Well, if they were to crack the safe, they might need to know this...

There are 10,000 possible combinations that the digits 0 to 9 can be arranged in to form a four-digit pin code that we all use at cashpoints or ATMs. But, of all the possible combinations, not all are used equally! If they were, then all PIN numbers would be used 0.2 per cent of the time and yet they are not.

The first reason is the influence of the 'repeaters'. These people repeat digits to create PIN numbers such as 1111, 3333, or 6666, as they are more easily recalled. Some, more advanced repeaters will go for slightly more complex repeats of 1212, or 8787, but none the less are categorised as the same group.

The second are the 'sequencers'. These are the people that look for patterns in the numbers to create a visual line along, across or down the keypad that you type the number into. Numbers like 1234, 9876 or 0852 (the straight line up the centre line of the key pad).

Or, are you in the third group, the 'daters'? This group like pin numbers that start with 19 or 20 as their first two numbers as these are dates of important birthdays, such as 1984 or 2006 (depending on either your age or the age of your children).

Combined, these three groups account for a very small proportion of the possible 10,000 PIN numbers but also account for the majority of PIN numbers used. In short, too many of us are repeaters, sequencers and daters!

Regardless of which heist member you are, your PIN number, whatever it is, gives you access to your money. It is the guardian of your cash. Without it you cannot withdraw a £10 note; with these digits, you can – assuming you have a reserve of cash in your account in the first place. Without an overdraft facility, despite still having a PIN number, you are not going to be able to access cash if it simply isn't there.

In a similar way, you may try to create everyday sums that just don't add up. You want to draw on your energy reserves when they have run dry and you want to withdraw against cognitive surplus when there is none available to draw upon. In short, you are running up too much credit and these loans will eventually need to be paid off; loans of sleep will need to be paid back; levels of energy will need to be recouped.

- **Are you too comfortable in taking out finance deals hoping that tomorrow will never come?**
- **Do you have an overdraft facility that will allow you to keep withdrawing?**
- **Can you spot the patterns of your predictable behaviour in this regard?**

In reality, you are in fact only stealing from yourself, pulling off your very own personal heist. It is wise to face the reality that, just as most of our PIN numbers are predictable, you too are predictable in your habits. You would be better off managing your overdraft facility and starting to balance your books. In most heists an alarm goes off, but you might not hear yours.

Invest the time to reflect on what your personal signals are that trigger when you've overspent. Most crucially, if you hear the alarm, don't ignore the warning.

25. WHEEL OF LIFE

The benefits of delayed gratification

- **Do you know what a zoetrope is?**

Prior to stop-frame animation, just before flip books started to entrance people by making the stationary seemingly move, there were zoetropes. A Victorian invention, the zoetrope was a thin cylindrical disc – rather like a narrow lampshade – on the surface of which was drawn a series of images that incrementally differed from each other. Over a sequence of 12 pictures, a horse would gallop or a clown could juggle. You watched this action through a series of narrow vertical slits that allowed you to witness this magic stroboscopic effect.

In order to achieve this illusion of movement, you had to rotate the zoetrope by turning a handle. This created the somewhat flickering image that appeared before your eyes. Within a rather limited timeframe, the sequence was over, but none the less it enthralled its Victorian audience. Indeed, in late 1867, a giant zoetrope with life-sized figures made an appearance at the same venue used for the Great Exhibition.

The word zoetrope is Greek in origin – with 'zoe' meaning life and 'trope' meaning turning. Essentially, these two words combined mean 'wheel of life'. Chrysalis to butterfly, tadpole to frog, seed to flower – life processes could be conveyed within the eight to 12 allowable images. This then made zoetropes an educational tool with the ability to fast-forward natural processes that take far longer in real life.

Maybe this was part of its enchantment – its ability to show such complex things in a way that was understood by the people who came to see it or were lucky enough to have their own.

Over 150 years later, people are still just as enthralled by speeding things up – trying to achieve something now, too soon, too quickly, with immediate results. However, in reality, you need to develop an affinity for delayed gratification. You need to learn to have the patience to wait for good things to come. In essence, it is better to enjoy the moment and to be captivated by what you see in front of you, just like our Victorian ancestors were when they saw the zoetrope.

- **How can you reconnect your modern self to a more measured, patient approach to life and its challenges?**

You may be guilty, like others, of not fully savouring the opportunities and experiences that you have. Always wanting the next thing, or to move onto something else, you are in danger of missing out on the now. In an attempt to get to the end, you may miss out on the journey that it takes to reach that point. Savouring the moment increases the enjoyment and boosts your happiness and this can have a significant and positive effect on your overall well-being and your resilience for tackling those next step challenges.

By deliberately focusing on the journey, the sense of movement, or the magic of change, you can become immersed in the joy of everyday life and linger in those moments more than you currently do. Safe in the knowledge that you are actually going to reach the final destination (after all, the zoetrope is a fixed circuit of images) you can relax and enjoy the evolutionary steps that it takes to reach that endpoint. In short, you will get the gratification, but in good time.

The changes required to achieve this may not come easily. However, like a zoetrope, you can set yourself incremental steps in order to reach it. You are in control of the handle that turns your cylinder; you can therefore better regulate the speed at which you turn it.

26. LENGTH TIMES WIDTH

Change your perception of what you can achieve

- **Imagine a dot. How many of these dots would it take to create a one-dimensional shape - a line?**

  2 dots

- **Imagine a straight line about 2 cm long. How many of these straight lines would it take to create a two-dimensional shape - a square?**

  4 lines

- **Imagine a square 2 cm long and 2 cm wide. How many of these squares would it take to create a three-dimensional shape – a cube?**

6 squares

- **Imagine a cube 2 cm long, 2 cm wide, 2 cm deep. How many of these cubes would you need to create a four-dimensional shape – a tesseract?**

8 cubes

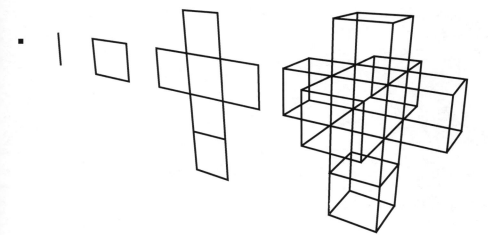

The pattern of the answers creates the sequence 2, 4, 6, 8. It builds up to eight cubes that make up the net of a tesseract.

- **Does this alter your previously perceived ideas of shapes?**

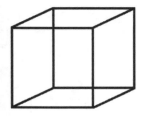

Now look at this shape from a different perspective.

- **What shape is this?**

A cube

- **The cube is made up of squares, but how many *actual squares* are in the picture above?**

Two

The other four 'squares' that make up this cube are illusions of squares. Over time, you have learnt that this is the way that you draw a square face of a cube on a piece of paper and therefore it looks familiar; yet it isn't a cube, just a 2D representation of one.

Now consider this: a 2D representation of that 4D shape called a tesseract.

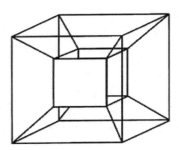

- **A tesseract is made up of cubes – but how many cubes can you see in this picture?**

Two (the big one and the little one inside it)

However, eight cubes make up a tesseract. So where are the other six?

Due to the tesseract being drawn on a piece of paper, it looks unfamiliar and wrong as we are not used to seeing it. However, through the process of drawing the shape on paper it has warped the other six cubes, so they look more like this:

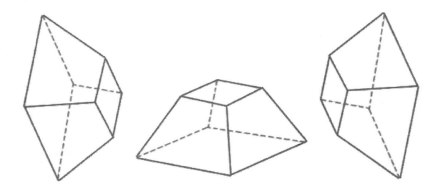

As in the previous example where the squares didn't look like squares, in this example, the cubes don't look like cubes either.

Hopefully, your perception has shifted from the childlike dot-to-dot to a more intellectual construct of cube-to-cube; from the well known to the less known. To push the limits of your perception, I deliberately started from an understanding with which you were already familiar and then built upon those firm foundations to push you further. Like a self-installed glass ceiling, your own perception may limit your exploration of new knowledge. Just by following the pattern of 2, 4, 6, you were able to get to 8; thereby following the path of the known, you were able to get to a lesser-known path.

Familiarity in the known is comforting. It is good to have a strong footing and to know where you are. Equally, change can be a good thing and can allow you to explore new areas of understanding. It can be risky, yet the opportunities that it can bring may well be worth that risk. If you remain curious about your environment, then that can boost your everyday experiences. Alternatively, by sticking with what you know, you risk limiting yourself, which in time can make you stagnant. This can have a negative effect on your self-esteem and this will reduce your overall resilience.

In conclusion, you can alter your perception, to stretch yourself, to expand your mind and allow alternatives to make themselves apparent. If you do, then your resilience will flourish and the everyday will become more engaging; the mundane will become enchanting.

27. GETTING TO THE ROOT OF THE PROBLEM

What you see on the surface is not the whole picture

The World Meteorological Organization publishes an International Cloud Atlas. First published in 1896, it is now an online resource that seeks to classify and name all known cloud formations. Indeed, they recently floated the idea of 11 new clouds which included futuristic names such as cataractagenitus (clouds that gather over a large waterfall) and silvagenitus (clouds that accumulate over so-called cloud-forests).

Set in the elevated dips between mountain peaks in countries such as Costa Rica, cloud-forests develop in unique meteorological conditions when there is permanent cloud cover, significant rainfall and high temperatures. These factors combine to generate the humidity that is perfect for plants such as mosses, ferns and epiphytes.

Epiphytes are highly specialised plants that are able to exist without soil. Such is the competition for space on the forest floor that these plants have relocated higher up the tree canopy in order to get the sunlight that they need. They have also adapted ways to survive on moisture from the air and nutrients from decomposing leaf litter that collects in the nooks and crannies of the joints between tree boughs. Sometime called air plants, particular species of orchids and bromeliads use their roots to anchor themselves to a branch.

However, less than 10 per cent of plant species have the highly evolved adaptability of an epiphyte. The vast majority of plants (the other 90 per cent) require the same root systems that you learnt about at primary school. Roots give anchorage, but also act as the main pathways for nutrients and water that are vital to sustain the plant. It is estimated that about 30 per cent of a shrub or tree is below ground, compared to 90 per cent of an iceberg being below water.

- **What percentage of a problem that you are faced with is hidden underground?**
- **Are you seeking to uproot this problem?**

If you look at an issue at work or at home, how much of it is exposed and obvious and what proportion is not immediately observable? It is only when you take the time to explore the issue more deeply that you begin to see the full depth of the problem – the complete whole, including the root system. This level of scrutiny is not easily achieved and takes time to hone. Pausing to reflect can, at times, be enough to shed the light needed on a particular issue. At other times, you need others to guide you to a greater understanding of it.

Alternatively, the issue you face needs to be exposed to the elements to ensure that your perception of it is accurate. This rational understanding will support you in making judgements that will lead to finding the necessary solutions, available options and potential routes forward. It will also allow you to filter out the facts from the fiction; the rational from the irrational. Once achieved, you will feel back in control, clear in the knowledge that you have dealt with the problem from its root base rather than superficially.

Root systems, whether in the ground, or in the air, provide anchorage and support. Sometimes you cannot see the hidden areas of the problems that you face. Locked onto the proportion that you can see, you can tend to block out the sections that you can't. At these times, you are vulnerable to misunderstanding the task in hand. However, you will know in yourself when you've fully uprooted the problem. This will alleviate the mental pressure and boost your confidence as a result. This can only help in raising your self-esteem and overall resilience.

28. FROGS AND MORTAR 💡

Build on firm foundations and add a brick at a time

- **Where are you most likely to hear the question *Frog up or frog down?***

  1) The Natural History museum

  2) A wildlife rescue centre

  3) From a 'brickie' on a building site

The answer is c. In an attempt to reduce the amount of clay being used per brick, while still retaining the structural integrity of this important building block, an indentation (called a frog) is created prior to the kiln phase of brick-making. This saves time as it uses less clay and is lighter to transport.

But why is this indentation called a frog? There are three main theories for consideration.

I. THE ANCIENT HISTORIAN

In ancient Egypt, it was customary to place a 'lucky frog' inside a brick that was being used within the construction of a pyramid. As an offering to the gods or as something that would be helpful in the afterlife, these creatures were sacrificed for the greater good of the pharaoh or other deceased individual.

2. THE EQUESTRIAN

In ancient brickwork pits, when the clay was directly dug from the ground, there were ponies that pulled their load of exhumed material. Their hooves made marks in the ground and these indentations formed clearly defined hoof-prints. The name of the cleft in a pony's hoof is called a frog and thus the name was connected to the manufacture of bricks.

3. GOING DUTCH

In order to create uniform brick sizes and shapes, and thus a stronger finished wall, the use of a brick mould is widespread. Older moulds were both wooden and had indentations called 'kickers' to kick the clay out to the edges. The English word was mistranslated into the Dutch word 'kikker' and this translates to frog!

Unfortunately, there is no definitive answer, as all are equally true. All that can be agreed upon is that, when bricks are placed 'frog up' they give greater structural integrity to the wall.

From strong foundations you can build your wall in everyday life.

- **What is the basis of a strong foundation for your wall?**
- **How do you achieve structural integrity within your wall?**
- **Which people do you need to bond with in order to bring them into your wall?**

Any foundation needs to be based on a sense of knowing who you are. From this starting point, you can begin to build others around you that complement your strengths or support you with your weaknesses or vulnerabilities. Built on trust, these chosen others can be bonded together to form your wall. Just like an English Bond or Flemish Bond brick pattern needs their required pattern of headers (short side of the brick) and stretchers (long side of the brick), you need to create a unique bond with others to bring them together.

From this firm, solid base you can then build your wall of connections that can help and support you in your life. Bonded together, they can collectively give you strength at times of need. By building from this solid base, you can place friends next to family, colleagues by partners, for layer upon layer.

However, building any wall takes patience and so does the building and maintaining of any relationship. Time is needed to place each brick and to ensure that it is level and bonded correctly in place. Indeed, it is the combination of time and trust that is integral to the quality of your wall. With time being such a premium in your life, you need to use it wisely and well. Allocating quality time to family and friends is always time well spent.

In short, considered construction over time will allow you to build higher and stronger than you ever thought possible. Whether it is trust, time or both, you need to decide who is needed to create the integral stability that you need to build your resilience, your inner strength.

29. SET-TOP TEACHING

Press pause to allow yourself a mental break

The 1950s advert for the first ever remote control for a domestic television stated: *You sit anywhere in the room... blissfully relaxed... with Zenith's wonderful Lazy Bones device in your palm.* It was connected to the TV by a wire and allowed you to change channels, adjust the volume and also turn it on and off. It was six years later before this remote was superseded by Space Commander TV. This time, the company described the device as: *The remote-control unit that tunes TV by silent sound.*

Indeed, these ultrasonic remotes became standard issue for TVs until the 1980s, when remotes began using infrared light signals instead of direct connection to the television unit. It was a Canadian company called Viewstar who created the device that allowed the low-frequency light beams to operate various electronic products.

Maybe this could have been called the Lazier Bones remote?

These days, commands can be spoken to our TVs which, by Bluetooth connection, can perform the required functions. The Bluetooth signal is actually a very short-distance radio signal, so in effect, it's reverting to the sound commands that the earlier remote controls used.

Maybe this could be called the Laziest Bones remote?

However, whatever remote you are using, similar features are now classed as standard across them all. You are now able to fast-forward the adverts, to record multiple programmes at the same time and to pause live TV. All stored on your set-top box to watch later, you create endless programme options to catch up with in the future.

Of all the features on a remote, the pause option is the most useful in terms of resilience, yet it is the one that is the most underutilised of them all. However, this feature allows you to stop what you are watching and pause it until you are ready to restart. These are the pauses that you need to put into your daily routines, to stop what you are doing and to consider where you need to go next. These temporary stops include sitting down for a while, relaxing for a bit, simply catching your breath.

- **What do you find is a good way to get yourself to pause?**
- **Are you currently able to find pause moments within your day?**
- **How long do those pauses need to be?**

This new 'resilient remote' also has unrivalled connection. You will be able to connect directly with yourself, which will guide your thinking in what you want to do and what you need to do next. This advanced feature will allow you to tap into your inner thoughts and to consider better options, improved choices and upgraded decisions. Coupled with the pause button this can be doubly effective.

- **How does it make you feel once you have allowed yourself a pause moment?**
- **Are you more productive once you have stopped and paused?**
- **Do you find that, despite pausing, you still reach the goal within a similar timeframe?**

When you need it most, this remote allows you to make the right choices straight away, by pausing and taking stock. It can give you the confidence to know that rational, considered responses can be found. In turn, your self-esteem will be boosted, as will your overall resilience – your ability to rise to the challenges that you are facing. All this is possible with the pause feature. Giving yourself that moment to consider your options is time well spent.

30. SKINNY, FLAT OR FULL FAT?

Ensure your teaching is the best that it can be

To most, coffee is either instant or filter, with milk or without, skinny or flat. However, throughout history, acorns, chicory and dandelions have all claimed to be worthy coffee substitutes.

If eaten raw, acorns have a really bitter taste, so it is important to process them before using them. Essentially, this entails drying, chopping and roasting them before preparing your brew. Tannin is the essential bitter-tasting element of the acorn (nature's way of protecting them from squirrels) but also crucial for that coffee-like flavour. White oak acorns are less tannin heavy and can therefore be used to make a more palatable drink.

While chicory doesn't contain any caffeine, it does share a similar flavour to coffee. For this reason, it has been used in times of war shortages to make a decent coffee substitute. Indeed, chicory was used as a component part of 'Camp Coffee', a liquid coffee substitute that was used to boost troop rations in the trenches of World War One. The thick black syrup proclaims to be a 'secret blend' of sugar, water, coffee and chicory essence.

Rather than the well-loved feathery white seed-head from our childhood, it is the dandelion root, not the flower, that is dried and then ground into coffee granules. These are then steeped in boiling water to produce the dandelion coffee substitute. It is supposed to have a similar taste to coffee but is slightly less bitter as it gains some sweetness from the natural sugars that are produced within the root. It doesn't contain any caffeine; resembling the taste, rather than the effect.

In essence, all three of these ingredients make coffee and yet, at the same time none of them are coffee. Indeed, they make a poor alternative for what we want our coffee to be. In a similar way, you may at times feel that your teaching can sometimes be a poor replacement for what you want it to be. Compromised by time, limited by subject knowledge or restricted by the behaviour of a child in your class, your teaching can sometimes be 'essence of teaching' rather than 'espresso teaching'.

There are three ways to get your teaching from 'medio' to 'grande':

- **connection;**
- **belonging; and**
- **empowerment.**

CONNECTION

If you are able to connect to your students and make the subject interesting then this will engage them as well as you. Your pupils need to believe that you care about them as individuals before they will engage. Once this condition is met, then extras can be added, the latte froth, in terms of making it fun and presenting your teaching in innovative ways.

BELONGING

If you are able to make pupils feel that they are an important part of their class and develop that sense of belonging in each of them, then this will reduce their anxiety and lead to increasing mental capacity for them, as well as greater opportunities to add creative flair for you. Once achieved, then learning will occur and academic progress will follow.

EMPOWERMENT

Third, if you are able to also underpin relationships in the classroom with trust, then you allow everyone to develop a sense of empowerment. When those in the learning space are given a sense of control over their learning, then this is hugely powerful. Self-motivation leads to driven students who want to do their best.

Combined, these three components of teaching become vital elements, the caffeine hit rather than the pretend compromises; the deep rich flavour rather than the pseudo-taste. They also create a closed loop mechanism that self-perpetuates resilient teachers who in turn are teaching more resilient children. People young and old need a sense of connection, a sense of belonging and a sense of empowerment to boost their resilience.

31. DO LESS, WELL

focus on one thing at a time and do that thing well

When, in 2003, Lynne Truss wrote the bestseller, *Eats, Shoots & Leaves: The Zero Tolerance Approach to Punctuation*, she made a panda wielding a gun a point of conversation for those who bought the book.

- **The difference was a comma; with eating shoots and leaves being the better-known panda activity.**

However, of equal interest were the uprisings in Russia, as opposed to the uprisings in China's panda population, to whom Truss dedicated her book. It was the striking printers of St Petersburg (and Moscow) who, in 1905, demanded to be *paid the same rate for punctuation marks as for letters* that Truss referred to.

In 1905, all across Russia, different groups of people were being moved into active protest, which would trigger a series of events that is now called the first Russian Revolution. The printers were joined by bakers, teachers, doctors, textile and machine tool workers, and even ballerinas. This all created an unplanned, yet shared aim: to improve their employment conditions by overthrowing the tsar.

In all, 60 per cent of workers went on strike, creating Soviets (workers' councils) all over Russia. Momentum against Tsar Nicholas II built up until he had to make concessions in a manifesto that, among other things, formed a Duma, a legally representative central assembly. This would eventually create the foundations for the Soviet Union 12 years later, when the line of supreme rulers, the monarchy of Russia, eventually came to an end.

- **But are commas worth fighting for?**
- **Can they really make that much difference?**

Consider the variance between these two pairs of sentences to see if they do.

Let's eat, Mum and *Let's eat Mum.*

- **The difference is a comma; with eating dinner with Mum rather than eating the maker of the dinner.**

Do less well and *Do less, well.*

- **The difference is a comma; the first appears to be asking for a lowering of performance, whereas in the second, it is asking for a rise in performance by concentrating on the task in hand.**

When faced with a multitude of work, you can feel overwhelmed and inadvertently become less effective and less efficient as a result. In an attempt to do everything well, you shift from one task to the next, then back again and you can end up not doing any of it well. Time spent focusing on one task at a time can considerably improve your overall output. You need to carefully manage your own individual productivity by giving the current task your undivided attention.

More resilient people develop strategies to focus on the task in hand rather than getting distracted by other jobs that are calling for their consideration. Breaks in your streams of consciousness make you less efficient and therefore all tasks take longer. Greater prioritisation of tasks and the time allocated to them is a skill that needs to be honed. If you are able to do this, then your productivity will improve and that can only be a good thing.

- **What interrupts the flow of your work at present?**
- **What steps do you proactively take to mitigate these interruptions?**
- **Who can help share the load of the task?**

This is not a stirring to create a coup or uprising. A comma is important and worth fighting for if that comma can teach you how to pause in the right places and reflect. Once you have worked out which is the most important task, then get on with it and get it completed to the best of your ability. By dealing with your present task you will progress to the next one more efficiently. Rather than doing the task 'less well', you will be 'more proficient'.

32. FEARFUL OF FAILING ⏱

fear of failure will stifle your chances to flourish

The NHS defines a phobia as *'an overwhelming and debilitating fear of an object, place, situation, feeling or animal'*. If you don't suffer from phobophobia, the fear of phobias, read on.

- **What do you think hippopotomonstrosesquipedaliophobia is the fear of?**

Long words.

Itself a collation of three words (hippopotamus, monstrous and sesquipedalian) this deliberately elongated word is a construction of big things. A hippo is obviously a huge creature; anything monstrous is larger than life; and that just leaves the Latin word. In its own right, sesquipedalian can itself be broken down into three constituent parts that come together to form a word that means 'a foot and a half long': sesqi – one and a half; ped – 'foot'; alian – the suffix that joins the two parts together.

If you previously didn't suffer from hippopotomonstrosesquipedaliophobia (35 letters), you may dislike long words after that explanation and yet not have a debilitating fear of them.

Importantly, the NHS definition of a phobia also includes the word *overwhelmed*. When things get too much, you can feel out of control. You lose your composure and the fight or flight instinct kicks in soon after. Under pressure, you crumple rather than relax into challenging situations. This is when you are prone to suffer from another phobia – atelophobia (11 letters), the fear of not being good enough. Not quite as lengthy as other phobias previously mentioned, this phobia is, however, much more widespread within the teaching profession.

Atelophobes often feel that everything they do is wrong. They have lost their confidence in what they do and how they do it. They feel that they are not good enough.

- **Does this sound familiar to how you sometimes feel in the classroom?**

Like many phobias, this may be an unrealistic perception of reality (as many phobias are) but for the people who are suffering from it, it feels very real. Many teachers will go to great lengths to avoid the feelings of atelophobia but this is not as easy as to achieve on a daily basis.

- **What do you do to avoid the feelings of not being good enough?**

Specific phobias are treated with exposure therapy where the person is introduced to the situation until the fear resolves itself. Gradual exposure to the feelings makes them realise that they are going to be OK. Feeling a renewed sense of empowerment, they can then learn to redefine themselves and their personal targets. Observations become less daunting; the inspector calling becomes less overwhelming.

- **Can you recall how you overcame a negative experience and made it 'right' the second time?**

Maybe the 'cure' of atelophobia is to be able to identify your strengths? If you can recognise the fact that all humans are flawed and imperfect, then you are better placed to accept your weaknesses but concentrate on your strengths. You need to try to feel less fearful of your weaknesses, and not to become phobic of your areas of development. After all, we all have them, we all have to deal with them.

So, rather than suffering from atelophobia, you need to start to discover your strengths (9 letters) rather than weaknesses; after all, 'strengths' is a Guinness World Record holder in a longest word category (with only one vowel, it is the longest one-syllable word).

- **What are your key strengths? Can you name three of them?**

In order to boost your resilience, develop a more realistic and balanced view of yourself. You, like everyone else, have to overcome your inner doubts, your fear of not performing under scrutiny, or the pressure you feel when your teaching is being observed. Maybe, it is your time to flourish, rather than to not be good enough?

33. THE KEYSTONE EXPERIENCES

Share the stress – what you can learn from the construction of arches

To address the water demand for Ancient Rome, the city's first aqueduct, named the Aqua Appia, was commissioned in around 312 BCE. However, as demand kept growing, a second aqueduct, the Aqua Anio Vetus, was constructed about 60 years later. It was able to transport more than twice the amount of water as the Aqua Appia. Impressively, it also entered the city on raised arches, so it would certainly have been dramatic for the locals.

By the late third century CE, the city was supplied with water by 11 state-funded aqueducts. This seems excessive, but the demand for water was there for local spas, pools and baths. Indeed, in the fourth century, Rome itself had more than 850 pools and baths, which only existed because of the expanded water supply from the ever-increasing number of water-carrying bridges – aqueducts.

However, the problems of water reserves were not just in Italy. As the Roman Empire expanded, so did the need for water to be channelled into the cities that they were overthrowing. In Spain, the aqueduct of Segovia had two layers of arches, 167 of them, to bring in their water. Going one better, with triple-layer arches, was the French Pont du Gard. This boasted six arches, topped by 11 arches, topped by a further 35 smaller arches.

Each of these arches were constructed 'un-mortared', ie with no mortar between the stones, and yet they still stand today as a testament to the Roman workers and craftsmen. Each and every arch also has a keystone – a pivotal stone at the apex of each of the arches – that locks all the other stones into place. As the final piece of the jigsaw, it enables the whole arch to cope with the stresses put upon it. Once you have one arch, then another can be built, either next to or on top of the other.

No matter if it is a Minoan, Roman or modern arch, the building principles remain the same. Essentially the stones distribute the stresses and the load between them, sharing it out between the springers (the base stones), the voussoirs (the building blocks) and the keystone at the apex. Carefully placed, each stone plays its role within the collective whole. Get it right and the arch can withstand these pressures for hundreds if not thousands of years.

Consider now which people make up the elements of your arch. Who are the people who help to support you and bolster your resilience within the workplace and at home?

- **Who are the springers in your life?**
- **Who are your voussoirs that build you up?**
- **Who is the keystone in your arch?**

Your springers could be the people who keep your feet on the ground. They could also be your family and friends who push you in the right direction. They are the foundation stones, the people who know you best, who can empathise, sympathise and sometimes constructively criticise. Without them you are not able to take on the stress and strains of everyday life.

- **Who are they for you?**

The other wedge-shaped stones that make up the arch are called voussoirs. These are the people who help to support you in your daily life. They help to share the stresses and to keep you on the right trajectory. Essentially, their guidance allows you to reach your goal, your zenith, the apex of your arch. They are crucial in helping you to manage the weight of your work.

- **Who are they for you?**

In reality, despite the help and support from others, you are the one who is pivotal in the management of your mindset – you are the keystone in your arch. Ultimately, only you have control of the way that you react to the strains of everyday life and manage your emotions, feelings and moods. While others can and will support you in this quest, you have final responsibility to hold up your arch of resilience!

Useful websites

www.britannica.com/topic/Segovia-aqueduct
www.britannica.com/topic/Pont-du-Gard
https://henlelatinclass.files.wordpress.com/2013/08/aqua-appia-ca-312-bc.jpg

34. THE SYCAMORE SPIN 🧭 👁

How feeling in a spin will end when you come back down to earth

There are two things that sycamore trees are famous for: the less-well known Welsh tradition of lovespoons and the popular, winged seed helicopters of your childhood.

Traditionally carved from one piece of wood, lovespoons are made from sycamore, but can also be honed from yew, oak, boxwood or lime. Dating from around 1670, young suiters would toil over a piece of sycamore, carving out hearts for love, entwined Celtic knots signifying together forever, or a key indicating their first home together. The love-struck male would then offer this slaved-over gift as a token of his commitment, dedication and affection.

The more well-known connection to the deciduous, native tree, however, is their paired samaras, the botanical name for the spiralling seed pods that fascinate children. Wind pollinated, the innovative design of the sycamore seed means air is pushed along the blades, the two arms get pushed in opposite directions, which in turn makes the seed pod twirl.

By this method, the sycamore seeds are able to fall far away from the mother tree, so they have plenty of space to grow and develop into the trees of the next generation. Indeed, if a sycamore tree was in the middle of a field, an acre in size, you may well find seedlings right up the edge of that space. In this way, the species is able to advance, and claim new ground with less competition for space, sunlight and nutrients.

A spinning sycamore seed is entrancing to watch. In a relatively short journey time, this seed has propelled itself to new ground, given itself fresh prospects and exciting opportunities for future growth. Rather than spinning out of control, it is a very precise rotation that is both purposeful and effective.

- **Have you ever felt that you are spinning out of control?**
- **How did that spinning sensation make you feel?**
- **Did you see it as a positive or negative experience?**
- **Looking back, can you see that it propelled you onto better things?**

On reflection, the short-term feelings of being unbalanced, unsteady and unsure are worthwhile for the longer-term benefits; the latent opportunities to better your circumstances. It can reignite your curiosity to explore new areas, and this level of intrigue is both exciting and empowering. Potentially this can create new meaning in your life and give a renewed purpose to it; you not only have survived the spin but are flourishing as a result of going somewhere new.

Now in a place where you can flourish, you begin to bear fruit – you can forget the spin – you are grounded and secure. With renewed confidence, you have become more resilient; stronger as a result of the change. You can rise to the challenges that you are set, safe in the knowledge that you are increasingly robust.

You can't change the unchangeable – you can't stick the samaras back on the tree. Neither can you stop the seeds from spinning and turning, or from moving onto fresh pasture. However, you can learn that sometimes, when you feel in a spin, you will come back down to earth soon enough. If you do, you may well be in a better place, one where you can flourish and grow. The short-term spin is worth it as you have been propelled onto better things.

35. RESERVOIR RESERVES ⏱

Hold something back for those 'just in case' moments

- **Can you name the five longest rivers in the world?**

    1) Nile (6,550 km) in Egypt

    2) Amazon (6,400 km) in South America

    3) Yangtze (6,300 km) in China

    4) Mississippi (6,275 km) in North America

    5) Yenisei (5,539 km) in Russia

Collectively, these five rivers have 31,064 km of flowing water across the major continents of the planet. Each is perfect for harnessing energy in order the meet the daily energy demands of humans. To help with this requirement, each of these rivers has a dam: the Nile's Aswan Dam; the Amazon's Belo Monte Dam; the Yangtze's Three Gorges Dam; the Mississippi's No. 15 (Rock Island) Dam; and the Yenisei's Krasnoyarsk Dam.

Dams are designed to harness the energy of controlled, falling water in order to generate electricity. Essentially an impervious wall, the dam creates a reservoir store behind it. When electricity is required, a certain amount of water is released, which rotates a turbine, that in turn generates the electricity – enough energy for over one and a half million homes.

These reservoirs are vast – the Aswan Dam, for example, holds 132 cubic kilometres (km^3) of water. If you consider that each km^3 is as large as 400,000 Olympic-size swimming pools this will go some way to help you conceive the enormity of the amount of water that is being dammed.

In a similar way, your overall resilience relies on a controlled flow to ensure that what you are expending is sustainable. Just as owners of dams employ people to constantly monitor water levels, you should apply the same level of self-monitoring to your energy levels.

- **What lessons can be learnt from dams?**
- **How are you able to build up reserves to call upon when you need them?**
- **How can you hold something back for the future if levels have not been replenished?**
- **What strategies can you employ to sustain your overall resilience?**

First, by managing the outflow of your resources, you are more likely to be able to maintain yourself for longer before you become depleted and less effective as a result. Releasing too much before lunchtime leaves you with too little for the afternoon sessions; letting out too much by Wednesday leaves you with minimal levels for the rest of the week.

- **Are you proactively managing your energy resources?**

Second, you would be wise to retain enough energy for those 'just in case' moments. You can't always plan for the unexpected, despite change sometimes feeling like the only constant that you can expect in your life. Life is both dynamic and changeable, so the need to have these reserves becomes all the more important. However, it is one thing to know about needing to take stock, but quite another to actually achieve it.

- **Are you retaining enough energy for those 'just in case' moments?**

Finally, you need to monitor your reserves in order to be able to draw upon them when needed. If you have depleted yourself by not carefully managing your energy levels, then you may leave yourself vulnerable. The result could be a lack of overall effectiveness or that you become ill and need to take time off work in order to recuperate.

- **How are you actively monitoring your energy levels?**

From Egypt to South America, from Russia to China, people have learnt to harness the power in the flow of our major rivers. You also need to harness your optimum power by giving more consideration to managing, retaining and monitoring your own reserves. This takes practice, time and investment. However, your overall resilience relies on you doing all three of these self-management tasks on a regular basis. It gives you enough energy and potentially helps those around you too.

36. RUCKSACK REQUIREMENTS ⏱

Coping with the weight of responsibility that you carry around

Imagine that you are about to set off on a heist. You have a rucksack with a limited capacity, so you need to select what you are going to steal carefully. You will be judged by the Boss on the value of the items that you have at the end of the job and there are too many items to be able to take them all. Constrained by this, you plan carefully, only selecting exhibits that will prioritise profit.

	EXHIBIT A	EXHIBIT B	EXHIBIT C	EXHIBIT D	EXHIBIT E	EXHIBIT F
VALUE	12K	6K	10K	5K	7K	4K
WEIGHT	10 KG	4 KG	8 KG	3 KG	5 KG	2 KG

Your backpack is limited to 10 kg – if you were theoretically allowed to select any exhibits, which combination would you steal? Remember, there is only one of each exhibit.

- **Exhibit A would get you to exactly the 10 kg limit and earn you £12,000.**

- **Exhibits C (8 kg) and F (2 kg) would earn you £14,000 (10k and 4k respectively).**

- **Exhibits B, D and F? Despite only weighing 9 kg, it brings in a haul of £15,000.**

- **Exhibits D, E and F? This weighs exactly 10 kg, but it brings in a haul of £16,000. You have hunted down the best bounty!**

'Constrained optimisations', also known as 'Rucksack problems', are puzzles that logistics and other companies are managing all of the time – from loading a ship with containers, to filling up a lorry with parcels and letters, to meeting the nutritional requirement for a space voyage where management of weight is crucial. Within tight time constraints, you may feel pressured to make decisions that are ultimately less productive and effective. Careful consideration of the task in hand can begin to mitigate the impact of this.

Ultimately, your rucksack has a limited capacity in your daily life too and as such needs to be managed. Not able to do all and everything, you have to calculate which combination of tasks will bring the greatest reward. Prioritisation is the key to optimisation and yet this is not something that comes easily to most people. With a quantity of emails to answer, letters to write, bills to pay, you can easily become overwhelmed and thus your mental state can deteriorate. Rather than doing something, you end up doing nothing, which inadvertently wastes precious time and subsequently increases the pressure you are under.

Alarms start to go off, you fear that you are going to get caught out, or at the very least that you are going to be found off-guard; all of which can have debilitating effects on your overall resilience. You need to do all that you can to mitigate this. You need to know, like the original rucksack problem at the start of this chapter, that it's easier to step back and break things down. Once you have this realisation, the maths problem becomes easier and the real-life problem does too. Rather than packing too much in, you need to consider what the optimal solution is for you at this time.

By planning the logistics before you get started you can maximise the impact of the work that you are able to complete within the finite timeframe that you have got. By working through your list, you can clarify the tasks that must, should and could be completed within the given timeframe. You could even rank their importance and estimate the time each is likely to take. This offers a more realistic, considered approach that should pay dividends, increasing your overall productivity, which will have a direct and positive link to your resilience. Just like the original rucksack problem had one optimal solution, maybe your job list does too?

37. MIX AND MATCH

Actively listening to improve communication with others

- **Did you know that noise-reducing headphone technology has developed a way to create sound waves that are the direct opposite of the noises around you, to allow you to actively listen to your music or audio book?**

Picked up by a built-in microphone, these headphones are then able to create this neutralising effect (an 'anti-sound') that allows for up to 70 per cent of ambient noise to be effectively blocked. This means that noise + noise = less noise. The two noises cancel themselves out – perfect for plane flights, train rides and other journeys.

- **Wouldn't it be good if you could employ a similar strategy in your professional life?**

Similarly, with headphones on, the skill of DJs is to be able filter out the information that they need – the beat of music, the tone of the song – so that they can be mixed together to form a coherent whole.

There would be an opening song, followed by others, before the finale. These 'joins' are pleasing for both the DJ and those in their audience.

Would you like to be able to hone in on the key communications at work and mix and match the important messages?

Known as crossfading, the DJ is able to transfer from one song to the other in a smooth transition of beats, tones or rhythms. However, they don't always get the right songs to fit together first time and this is known as 'dropping' in DJ circles. Inadvertently, this can create something that would be described as a cacophonous (harsh) rather than a euphonious (pleasing) sound.

Wouldn't it be good if you could avoid 'dropping' your communication links in everyday life?

Like DJs, you are able to tune into the nuances of a conversation and pick out key information in order to be able to make connections between the words and phrases being used. Skilled listeners are able to pick out that key information and then reflect that back to the speaker. This builds empathy and is a skill that you need to harness and hone in order to build your own resilience. Too often you don't hear what is being said as your interpretation is tarnished by your filters of who has said it and how it is being said, as much as what is being said.

However, the skill of active listening takes patience and skill to develop, just like a DJ practising to improve their mixing. The ability comes from being able to transition between hearing and listening; the ability to hear sounds is a blessing, but the ability to interpret those same sounds is a skill that needs to be refined. In this way, you take in more accurate information, which in turn improves your perception of reality. Subsequently, this allows you to be confident and more self-assured as you know that you are hearing things objectively. If you can achieve this then you will inevitably be more resilient as a result.

Active listening is one of the best communication tools that you possess, and it can improve your connections with other people. It also promotes a level of respect for the person, which means that you will get the best from them and vice versa. It can also encourage both parties to use their time together effectively and be more productive as a result. By fully immersing yourself in a conversation, you pick up the key information that can inform future actions and decisions, clear in the knowledge that you know what needs to be done. These conditions are perfect for creating a resonant match with others; the perfect mix for your resilience.

38. JOB LIST SHUFFLE 💡

Prioritise your workload and get started with that first job

When the second-generation iPod Shuffle first appeared on the market in 2006, its diminutive size (around 3 cm × 4 cm × 1 cm) belied the fact that this wearable technology was going to introduce a new element to our music listening. This randomisation meant that you no longer listened to track one followed by track two. Instead, you could listen to track three from album five and then track four from album six. This negated the need for display units as the element of choice was also effectively removed. Instead, the iPod Shuffle would select which track to play next from the songs that you had uploaded onto it.

The Wurlitzer 1015, which is the quintessential jukebox, became a big hit in 1946. Four years later, Wurlitzers were capable of holding up to 100 vinyl 45s, which allowed for a wide range, yet limited number, of songs to be played. After paying with your coins, you could choose which of the songs the people in the room, including yourself, would listen to next. You therefore had some control over the playlist, but not total control.

Modern radio stations too have a limited number of songs that they play. The variety of songs played by the radio station will differ significantly according to the audience to whom they are marketed. Priority will be given to that week's popular songs, while last week's will slowly drift from being played hourly, to daily, to weekly. In this way, you choose the radio station, yet the DJ chooses the order of songs played.

All three musical inventions have allowed you to listen to your favourite music. From the dance halls of the 1950s to music-accompanied jogs in 2006 to the kitchen being filled with songs from digital radios in 2019, all have an element of choice; all have an element of control. In your daily life, you also have 'playlists' to complete. You call them job lists or work lists, but essentially they contain a list of the tasks that you have left to complete at work, at school or at home. Faced with this multitude of duties, you have a choice.

- **Take the iPod Shuffle approach**

  This involves uploading daily tasks each day and then working your way through them in any order. Randomising these jobs may help to make a quick choice so that the job itself can get started rather than dithering about which to do next.

- **Take the jukebox approach**

  Here you have some choice about which job to do next. However, sometimes you will be in the control of others who will name the job that you need to do. The benefits/risks of this are that you are likely to just repeat the tasks you like and never get onto the others that don't appeal yet still need to be completed.

- **Take the 'Job list FM' approach**

  Safe in the knowledge that priority will be given to this week's popular jobs, you can listen knowing that what others are suggesting should be your priorities – for example, a directive from the head teacher. By responding to the DJ's choices, you are able to keep up with important jobs by following others' leads.

It is not easy to decide which approach is needed on a day-to-day basis. However, each can enable you to be in charge of the choices that you have. This can be empowering but also more productive too as you know that you are on the right playlist; you just need to get started.

How enjoying the journey will lead to a positive ending

- **Can you name an animation in which Cinderella and Pinocchio both appear?**

Shrek

The loveable ogre lives with his trusty donkey until his home gets swamped by fairy tale characters from childhood stories including Cindy (as she was called in the film) and also Geppetto's famous creation, Pinocchio. The ending is suitably fairy tale in that Princess Fiona, despite not being changed into a princess by Shrek's kiss, is still his princess on the inside. While this is all happening, Donkey, voiced by Eddie Murphy, starts to sing 'I'm a Believer'. This raises the question, is it reality to believe that situations will always end positively?

Certainly, the suitably whimsical 'happy ever after' ending has become the stock, almost formulaic, phrase, that comes at the end of fairy tales and many of the early Disney movies. As the end credits roll, we feel a sense of relief that all is well for our characters and that they (and we) are left content: Cinderella eventually gets her slipper back; Pinocchio fulfils his dream to become a real human boy; Shrek gets his ogress.

Less well known is the conversation in *The Fellowship of the Ring*, the first in the Lord of the Rings books, where Bilbo asks Frodo, '*Have you thought of an ending?*' to which Frodo replies, '*Yes, several, and all are dark and unpleasant*'. Almost foretelling the adventures to come, there is a sense of wise prophecy here. Rather like the Snakes and Ladders board in Chapter 2, there are going to be trials and tribulations along the journeys you take. But isn't it these adventures that make the film? Even Disney's fairy tale retellings have some misfortunes for Snow White and Sleeping Beauty along the way.

So, are you a *believer*, with *not a trace of doubt in your mind*, in happy endings? Well, I believe that you are more in control than you think, in terms of creating a happ*ier* ending for yourself. When reflecting on how good things have been at the end of the day, week or term, you can make better, more informed choices about your perception of challenges and your responses to them. Resilient individuals, if they employ some of the strategies suggested in this book, will more likely be happ*ier* as they rise to the challenges before them and bounce back from the adversities when they inevitably come.

By getting to this point in the book, you have read a wealth of information taken from everyday life that can remind you of the holds that you can reach for when you're climbing life's beanstalk. There is no ring, or dragon sitting on a hoard of gold, at the end of this book. I cannot offer you such reward. However, what I have offered you, in this and the previous chapters, are the tools for improved mental wealth. We have been on a 'journey' of 39 steps, and hopefully the self-learning that you have achieved along the way has made you stronger and more resilient. If you follow the advice given in this book then you most certainly have a better chance of having a happ*ier* ending to your month, your week, your year! I hope that I have encouraged you to be a believer – to believe in yourself and your capacity to do ever-more amazing things.

Look out for other books in this series!

See www.criticalpublishing.com for more details.

FUTURE PROOF YOUR SCHOOL
steering culture, driving school improvement, developing excellence

Wouldn't it be great if you could equip your school and yourself to face whatever the future might throw at you?
Schools face myriad calls on their time and creativity yet have finite internal resources to respond to them. This book reduces, filters and prioritises the demands on staff energy to the central task of all schools – to achieve the best engagement of and learning outcomes for all learners (including the staff themselves). It is suitable for headteachers, senior or aspiring leaders, and those driving change through initiatives, but also individual teachers who are interested in effective practice as a route towards personal well-being and professional satisfaction.

ISBN: 978-1-912508-44-0

SHIFTING SANDS
contemporary issues in primary education

Do you feel as if the ground beneath your feet is constantly shifting?
It's not surprising if you do! Teachers today are faced with a range of complex, current issues that impact on teaching and learning, as well as the need to understand and address a raft of new initiatives, directives and policy changes. This accessible book gives you all the information in one place, unpicks key elements of legislation and policy, and suggests practical approaches and resources that could be used in the classroom to successfully address the issues.

ISBN: 978-1-912508-53-2